Celebrate King Jesus

A Chronological Study of the Book of Revelation

DR. BONNIE L. WESTHOFF

WestBow Press books may be ordered through booksellers or by contacting:

WestBow Press
A Division of Thomas Nelson & Zondervan
1663 Liberty Drive
Bloomington, IN 47403
www.westbowpress.com
1 (866) 928-1240

Bible abbreviations are taken from *Strong's Concordance*.

All definitions in *Vine's Complete Expository Dictionary* (of Old Testament Hebrew and New Testament Greek) are taken as exact excerpts to protect the validity of the resource. Information in brackets [] is added to quoted text by the author.

ISBN: 978-1-5127-4098-1 (sc)
ISBN: 978-1-5127-4099-8 (hc)
ISBN: 978-1-5127-4097-4 (e)

Library of Congress Control Number: 2016907138

Print information available on the last page.

WestBow Press rev. date: 7/28/2016

Acknowledgments

I'd like to thank my friend Sherry Brandel for being one in the Holy Spirit with me. When my husband, Ronnie, passed away six years ago, Sherry stayed with me the first three days because she knew my inner thoughts and helped me make so many decisions during that difficult time. She was there for me when Ronnie had his heart attack, and she took me to the hospital. They were not able to resuscitate him, so he went separately in the rescue vehicle. When at the hospital they asked me if I wanted to see the body, I automatically said no; I didn't think I could do that. Sherry automatically said yes; she wants to see him. She went with me to say my good-byes. I will be forever thankful.

Since then, she has called me daily to make sure I am all right. But it is more than that. We are unified in our love for Jesus, and she has such wisdom that it's as if the Holy Spirit confirms everything He tells me through her.

On the way home from the hospital, I asked God for the purpose in all this; how was I to honor my husband in this loss? I told Sherry my life goal was to give glory to Jesus in everything I did as a result of Ronnie's absence. Now, I celebrate that my calendar is sold out to Jesus and I am doing so much more today than ever.

Sherry motivates me by getting excited about all the things I do. The Bible says that when we get to heaven, we will receive a crown in appreciation for all the things we did through the Holy Spirit on earth. We laugh when we tell each other that we will ask Jesus if she and I can share a crown; we will tell Him it will have to fit on both our heads because she is so much a part of everything I do. I wouldn't be publishing this book if it weren't for her wanting to experience what I had learned.

Our friends are treasures Jesus sends to make us laugh when we go through bad experiences and cry when we experience something too good to be true. Thank you, Sherry, for being a friend who laughs and cries with me, gets me through the bad, and celebrates the good with me. You are a treasure God sent to me. I love you dearly and appreciate your husband, Joe, for promoting our togetherness and helping with tasks that are far too big for me. Thank You, Jesus, for friendships!

Praise You, Jesus!

Contents

Introduction

John the apostle wrote Revelation just prior to the turn of the century, before AD 100. He was exiled to the island of Patmos (Rev 1:6) where the Lord gave him visions of the following:

- chapter 1: things you have seen (victory of the resurrection of Christ)
- chapter 2–3: things that are (victory of the church age)
- chapter 4–22: things that will take place (victory of Christ's rule)

John's gospel brought forth redemption for the inhabitants of the earth at the first coming of Christ, and the book of Revelation brought forth the judgment for those who reject Christ's redemption. Anyone who rejects the Lord throughout time will be judged by Jesus Christ (Ro 2:3).

Chapter 1 begins with John seeing Jesus on the throne of God after His resurrection. This is to let the church know He is there as the head of the church, the Lord of Glory seated as our High Priest. John was told these were the things that you have seen. In John's day, this had already happened.

Chapters 2 and 3 depict the church age, things in the present time for all who read the Word. This will continue until the church is raptured.

Chapter 4 opens with the church, the lampstands in 1:20 around the throne of God. That means the church has been raptured.

Chapter 5 finds only Christ worthy to open the seals that show His inheritance contract—earth belongs to Him. It was only temporary for Satan to rule the world. Genesis 3:15 was a promise that Satan's reign would end.

Chapter 6 is the rise of the Antichrist after the restrainer, the church, has been raptured.

Chapter 7 shows Christ sealing God's people, those living in the tribulation who have seen the truth of God's Word. God will always protect a remnant of His people (Ro 9:27).

Chapters 8 through 19 are the seven-year tribulation. In heaven, Jesus is crowned King and comes to earth to be victorious in the Battle of Armageddon. His church, the bride of Christ, comes with Him in their glorified bodies to rule and reign throughout the millennium. Satan is thrown in the bottomless pit during the thousand-year reign.

Chapter 20 covers the millennium. I don't see where anyone dies during that period. I don't see sickness during the millennium reign as was the case during the forty years in the wilderness when God protected His people.

During the millennium reign, the earth will be repopulated as it was in the time of Noah. The millennium ends by allowing Satan to be released, at which time he convinces many who were born during this period to rebel against Christ. At the great white throne judgment, all nonbelievers, followers of Satan, will be judged and will spend eternity in the lake of fire.

Chapters 21–22 show God's people living harmoniously in His divine love. Everything Satan corrupted is restored new; then God's plan is complete.

The program of God culminates in Revelation. God's plan was for us to know Him and dwell with Him. God has been long-suffering; He has given every generation the opportunity to come to Him and make their dwelling place with Him (Col 1:23). No one knows the day or the time when Christ will come for His church (Mt 24:36), but that will kick off the tribulation in Revelation.

The Greek word for *revelation* is *apokalypsis*. We refer to it as the Apocalypse, meaning "the unveiling." The word is singular, referring to only one person who will be revealed: Christ. Throughout the New Testament, we see Jesus as our Savior, but He will come to receive His inheritance as the King. Here, the holy Jesus will be revealed on the throne of God and the judgment promised in the Bible will occur.

Revelation is a difficult book because everything God said in the Bible has already been prophesied. Prophesies from Isaiah, Jeremiah, Ezekiel, Daniel, Joel, Amos, Zechariah, and Jesus Himself all culminate in this end-time book. Amos wrote, "Surely the Lord God does nothing unless He reveals His secret to His servants the prophets" (Am 3:7). Therefore, my intent is to reference Scripture throughout this commentary that prophesied each event. God is not a God of surprises.

Throughout the introduction, the following topics will be revealed for a better understanding of the book.

1. Revelation is a Book of Sevens
2. Revelation of Heaven and Hell
3. Revelation of the Satanic Trinity
4. Revelation of Satan's Plan
5. Revelation of the Five Judgments in Revelation
6. Revelation of the Tribulation That Begins at the Time of the Rapture of the Church
7. Revelation of the Seventy Weeks of Daniel

1. Revelation is a Book of Sevens

Revelation is a book of sevens. Seven is the number of completion.

- Rev 2: The seven churches
- Rev 4: The seven spirits of God
- Rev 6: The seven sealed judgments
- Rev 8: The seven trumpet judgments
- Rev 12: The seven people of the great tribulation
- Rev 15: The seven bowl (vial) judgments
- Rev 21: The seven new things

2. Revelation of Heaven and Hell

Since Revelation switches from heaven to earth and to hell rapidly, it is important to just briefly describe some terms.

The Hebrew for the word *heaven* is *shamayim*, a plural noun. Scripture reveals three heavens.

- The first heaven is the earth atmosphere: "Lord, when You went out from Seir, when You marched from the field of Edom, the earth trembled and the heavens poured, the clouds also poured water; the mountains gushed before the Lord, this Sinai, before the Lord God of Israel" (Jdg 5:4-5). The rapture will take place when Jesus returns in the clouds.
- The second heaven is the planetary system: "The heavens declare the glory of God; and the firmament shows His handiwork" (Ps 19:1). The spiritual wars are fought somewhere out in the firmament.
- The third heaven is God's dwelling place: "When they pray toward this place, then hear in heaven Your dwelling place; and when You hear, forgive" (1Ki 8:30). Here, we will find the throne room where all the angels are discharged to fight for Christ during the tribulation.

Scriptures that describe hell include the following:

- Ps 9:17: "The wicked shall be turned into hell, and all the nations that forget God."
- Isa 14:9–11: "Hell from beneath is excited about you, to meet you at your coming; it stirs up the dead for you, all the chief ones of the earth; it has raised up from their thrones all the kings of the nations. They all shall speak and say to you 'Have you also become as weak as we have, you become like us, your pomp is brought down to Sheol, and the sounds of your stringed instruments; the maggot is spread under you, and worms cover you.'"
- Isa 66:24: "And they shall go forth and look upon the corpses of the men who have transgressed against me. For their worm does not die, and their fire is never quenched. And shall be an abhorrence to all flesh."
- Mt 25:41: "Then He will also say to those on the left hand, 'Depart from Me, you cursed, into the everlasting fire prepared for the devil and his angels.'"
- Mt 25:46: "And these will go away into everlasting punishment, but the righteous into eternal life."

- 2Pe 2:4: "For if God did not spare the angels who sinned, but cast them down to hell and delivered them into chains of darkness, to be reserved for judgment."
- Rev 9:1–2: "Then the fifth angel sounded: And I saw a star fallen from heaven to the earth. And to him was given the key to the bottomless pit. And he opened the bottomless pit, and smoke arose out of the pit like the smoke of a great furnace. And the sun and the air were darkened because of the smoke of the pit."
- Lk 16:19–31: the parable of the rich man and Lazarus. Verse 22 says the rich man died and was in torment in Hades. In verse 26, there is a great gulf fixed so those who want to pass from Hades to paradise cannot, nor can those in paradise pass over to Hades.

When Jesus died and went to hell to take over Satan's authority, He emptied all the Old Testament saints from paradise, and they went to heaven with Jesus. Ephesians 4:8–10 says, "When He ascended on high, He led captivity captive, And gave gifts to men. (Now this, 'He ascended'—what does it mean but that He also first descended into the lower parts of the earth? He who descended is also the One who ascended far above all the heavens, that He might fill all things.)"

All saints who die today go to the third heaven, not paradise. When Jesus through His shed blood overcame Satan, He took legal authority and released all God's saints from eternity past to eternity future; Jesus died for all God's children, those who will enter the kingdom of God.

3. Revelation of the Satanic Trinity

The godly Trinity is Father, Son and Holy Spirit, and Satan copies everything God does. Revelation 20:10 depicts Satan as a trinity: "And the devil [Satan], who deceived them, was cast into the Lake of Fire and brimstone where the beast [Antichrist] and the false prophet [Antispirit] are."

4. Revelation of Satan's Plan

Any plan in opposition to God's plan is Satan's plan. Revelation 20:4 reads, "Then I saw the souls of those who had been beheaded for their witness to Jesus and for the word of God, who had not worshiped the Beast or his image, and had not received his mark on their foreheads or on their hands." These beheadings are part of radical Islam that opposes the God of Jews and Christians and calls them infidels. It is important to understand the beliefs of Islam.

1. Muhammad, the father of Islam, died in 632. There are three different faiths that developed under Islam.

    - Sunni (Iraq): Their doctrine is the Qu'ran.
    - Shi'a (Iran): The descendants of Muhammad were called imams. During the ninth century, the twelfth imam was said to have hidden; it is believed he will return with Jesus. Their doctrine is the Hadiths, which consists of the original sayings of the imams.
    - Wahhabism (Saudi Arabia): under Sunni; believe both the Qu'ran and Hadiths, and have also added a book on monotheism.

2. Five Pillars of Islam—agreed upon as essential for all three faiths.

    - Shahadah (creed): There is no God but Allah, and Muhammad is his prophet.
    - Salat (daily prayers): Prayer five times a day in direction of Mecca.
    - Zakah (almsgiving): Give alms to the power (2.5%) to imam or charity.
    - Sawm (fasting): Fast each day during Ramadan from sunrise to sunset.
    - Hajj (pilgrimage): pilgrimage to Mecca once during lifetime.

3. The Mahdi
    Muslims believe Abraham had two sons, Ishmael and Isaac. Isaac became the Jews, and Ishmael became the Islamic faith. The twelfth imam is called the Mahdi. In 2006, the tomb of the tenth and eleventh imams in a mosque in Samarra, Iran, was destroyed

supposedly to cause a civil war. One thousand Muslims died. The twelfth imam's mosque was not touched. They believe that when Christ returns, the Muslims will kill the Jews and rule and reign with Jesus Christ. They believe the Mahdi will rule seven years when the Antichrist appears, they will kill the Jews, and then world peace will come (Serah 4:159, 43:61 and sixteen Hadiths relating to Jesus). True peace for Islam is that the Jews and Christians, all infidels, must come under submission to Allah, their god. Ahmadinejad's effort for nuclear supremacy is to prepare for the twelfth imam. He believes that civil war will bring the Mahdi's return.

4. ISIS (Islamic State of Iraq and Syria)
This is a Sunni group that originated as jihad in 1999 and was renamed al-Qaeda in Iraq in 2004. By 2013, the group changed its name again to ISIL (Islamic State of Iraq and the Levant). Abu Bakr al-Baghdadi entered a civil war and today has a large presence in Syria and Iraq. Today, Amir al-Mu'minin has been named caliph and claims authority over all Muslims. Islam is the world's second largest religious group with 1.5 billion people and makes up 23 percent of the world's population.

We do not condone killing in the United States. Islam lives under Sharia law and approves of honor killing as an act of vengeance against anyone who has brought dishonor upon his or her family. Sharia is used as a basis for divorce and gaining inheritance. If Sharia law were to come to the United States, this law would protect terrorism and these honor killings. They could not be legislated under the government but instead would be classified as under religious jurisdiction.

The Qu'ran 2:191 says, "Fight in the cause of Allah those who fight you, but do not transgress limits; for Allah loves not transgressors. And kill them wherever you find them, and drive them out from whence they drove you out, and persecution is severer than slaughter, and do not fight with them at the Sacred Mosque until they fight with you in it, but if they do fight you, then slay them; such is the recompense of the unbelievers."

We see Shite Islam (Iran) taking over Sunni Islam (Syria and Iraq). As we see the tribulation break out, the Antichrist will seek a one-world rule, a one-world religion, and a one-world currency.

5. Revelation of the Five Judgments in Revelation

1. Bema seat judgment of Christ for believers
   The word *bema* is Greek and comes from the bema platform used by the judge in the Isthmian games in which contestants would compete for the prize. Victors would have wreaths placed on their heads. This judgment takes place after the rapture, when the church receives rewards for those things done through the love of Christ. It pictures the Lord our God as the consuming fire. Each judgment was prophesied in the Old Testament, prophesied through the Lord, and fulfilled in Revelation by our Lord Jesus.

   - Dt 4:24; Heb 12:29: "For the Lord your God is a consuming fire, a jealous God."
   - Jn 5:24: "Most assuredly, I say to you, he who hears My word and believes in Him Who sent Me has everlasting life, and shall not come into judgment, but has passed from death into life."
   - 1Co 3:11–15 (describes works being burned at the judgment): "For no other foundation can anyone lay than that which is laid, which is Jesus Christ. Now if anyone builds on this foundation with gold, silver, previous stones, wood, hay, straw, each one's work will become manifest; for the Day will declare it, because it will be revealed by fire; and the fire will test each one's work, of what sort it is. If anyone's work which he has built on it endures, he will receive a reward. If anyone's work is burned, he will suffer loss; but he himself will be saved, yet so as through fire."
   - Rev 5:11–14: "Then I looked, and I heard the voice of many angels around the Throne, the living creatures, and the elders; and the number of them was ten thousand times ten thousand, and thousands of thousands, saying with a loud voice: 'Worthy is the Lamb who was slain to receive power

and riches and wisdom, and strength and honor and glory and blessing!' And every creature which is in heaven and on the earth and under the earth and such as are in the sea, and all that are in them, I heard saying: 'Blessing and honor and glory and power be to Him who sits on the Throne, and to the Lamb, forever and ever!' Then the four living creatures said, 'Amen!' And the twenty-four elders fell down and worshiped Him who lives forever and ever."

2. Judgment of Jews during the tribulation
Jeremiah and Daniel call the tribulation the time of Jacob's trouble. During this time, the Jews will believe Jesus is the Messiah and become believers. This takes place during the first half of the tribulation until Jesus comes down and pronounces that He can delay their suffering no more (Rev 10:7).

- Jer 30:4–7: "Now these are the words that the Lord spoke concerning Israel and Judah. For thus says the Lord: 'We have heard a voice of trembling, of fear, and not of peace. Ask now and see whether a man is even in labor with child? So why do I see every man with his hands on his loins like a woman in labor and all faces turned pale? Alas! For that day is great and it is the time of Jacob's trouble, but he shall be saved out of it.'"
- Da 12:1: "At that time Michael shall stand up, over the sons of your people; and there shall be a time of trouble, such as never was since there was a nation, even to that time. And at that time Your people shall be delivered, everyone who is found written in the book."
- Mt 24:21–31: "For then there will be great tribulation, such as has not been since the beginning of the world until this time, no, nor ever shall be. And unless those days were shortened, no flesh would be saved; but for the elect's sake those days will be shortened. Then if anyone says to you, 'Look, here is the Christ!' or 'There!' do not believe it. For false Christ's and false prophets will arise and show great signs and wonders, so as to deceive, if possible, even the elect. See, I have told you

beforehand. Therefore, if they say to you, 'Look, He is in the desert! Do not to go out;' or 'Look, He is in the inner rooms!' do not to believe it. For as the lightening comes from the east and flashes to the west, so also will the coming of the Son of Man be. For wherever the carcass is, there the eagles will be gathered together. Immediately after the Tribulation of those days the sun will be darkened, and the moon will not to give its light; the stars will fall from heaven, and the powers of the heavens will be shaken. Then the sign of the Son of Man will appear in heaven, and then all the tribes of the earth will mourn, and they will see the Son of Man coming on the clouds of heaven with power and great glory. And He will send His angels with a great sound of a trumpet, and they will gather together His elect from the four winds, from one end of heaven to the other."

- Rev 10:1–7: "I saw still another mighty angel coming down from heaven, clothed with a cloud. And a rainbow was on his head, his face was like the sun, and his feet like pillars of fire. He had a little book open in his hand. And he set his right foot on the sea and his left foot on the land, and cried with a loud voice, as when a lion roars. When he cried out, seven thunders uttered their voices. Now when the seven thunders uttered their voices, I was about to write; but I heard a voice from heaven saying to me, 'Seal up the things which the seven thunders uttered, and do not write them.' The angel whom I saw standing on the sea and on the land raised up his hand to heaven and swore by Him who lives forever and ever, who created heaven and the things that are in it, the earth and the things that are in it, and the sea and the things that are in it, that there should be delay no longer, but in the days of the sounding of the seventh angel, when he is about to sound, the mystery of God would be finished, as He declared to His servants the prophets."

3. Judgment of nations against God and His people (sheep/goat judgment)
   A sheep/goat judgment determines who will live into the next phase of the end times. The sheep are believers in Jesus Christ as

the Son of God while the goats are unbelievers. The first sheep/goat judgment is in Revelation 20 prior to the return of Jesus for the second coming after the seven-year tribulation is over and before the Battle of Armageddon. This will determine the people who will live during the millennium.

The second sheep/goat judgment is after the millennium and before the war of Gog and Magog. Jesus will judge who will live into eternity and who will be thrown into the lake of fire. Each battle before the millennium and before eternity will not really be a battle. Satan will prepare for battle, and Christ our King will pronounce the sword of the Lord and those written in the Book of Life will be protected while those who are not will be slain. God knows the hearts of His people. Humanity will always condemn itself by rejecting the truth of the one true God.

- Joel 3:1–2: "For behold, in those days and at that time, when I bring back the captives of Judah and Jerusalem, I will also gather all nations and bring them down to the Valley of Jehoshaphat; and I will enter into judgment with them there on account of My people, My heritage Israel, whom they have scattered among the nations; they have also divided up My land."
- Mt 25:31–32: "When the Son of Man comes in His glory, and all the holy angels with Him, then He will sit on the Throne of His glory. All the nations will be gathered before Him, and He will separate them one from another, as a shepherd divides his sheep from the goats."

4. Judgment of Satan
Satan will be placed in the bottomless pit for one thousand years during the millennial rule of Christ. When he is released, he will cause the war of Gog and Magog and his judgment will be to finally send him to the lake of fire for eternity. Satan is used by God throughout time to test all creation to see if they will worship the one true God.

- Jn 5:26-27: "For as the Father has life in Himself, so He has granted the Son to have life in Himself, and has given Him authority to execute judgment also, because He is the Son of Man." God has given Jesus, His Son, authority to judge Satan.
- Rev 19:20: "Then the beast was captured, and with him the false prophet who worked signs in his presence, by which he deceived those who received the mark of the beast and those who worshiped his image. These two were cast alive into the Lake of Fire burning with brimstone."
- Rev 20:1-3: "Then I saw an angel coming down from heaven, having the key to the bottomless pit and a great chain in his hand, He laid hold of the dragon, that serpent of old, who is the Devil and Satan, and bound him for a thousand years; and he cast him into the bottomless pit, and shut him up, and set a seal on him, so that he should deceive the nations no more till the thousand years were finished. But after these things he must be released for a little while."
- Rev 20:10: "The devil, who deceived them, was cast into the Lake of Fire and brimstone where the beast and the false prophet are. And they will be tormented day and night forever and ever."

5. Great white throne judgment on all
   This final judgment in Revelation 20:11–15 by Christ is on all humanity ever born. The Antichrist, the Beast, and the False Prophet (the satanic trinity) will be thrown into the lake of fire forever (Rev 19:20). All the wicked will also go there forever.

- Da 7:26: "But the court shall be seated, and they shall take away his dominion, to consume and destroy it forever."
- Jn 12:48: "He who rejects Me, and does not receive My words, has that which judges him—the word that I have spoken will judge him in the last day."
- 2Pe 3:7: "But the heavens and the earth which are now preserved by the same word, are reserved for fire until the day of judgment and perdition of ungodly men."

- Rev 20:11–15: "Then I saw a great white throne and Him who sat on it from whose face the earth and the heaven fled away. And there was found no place for them. And I saw the dead, small and great standing before God, and books were opened. And another book was opened which is the Book of Life. And the dead were judged according to their works, by the things which were written in the books. The sea gave up the dead who were in it, and Death and Hades delivered up the dead who were in them. And they were judged, each one according to his works. Then Death and Hades were cast into the Lake of Fire. This is the second death. And anyone not found written in the Book of Life was cast into the Lake of Fire."

6. Revelation of the Tribulation That Begins at the Time of the Rapture of the Church

Are we ready for the rapture of the church? Only Christians will be caught up with Christ and escape the tribulation. To be a Christian, simply ask Jesus to forgive your sins. Acknowledge He is the Son of God, was born to save you from your sins, was crucified and resurrected, and is seated at the right hand of the Father in heaven.

Testimony from Jesus that He will return for those who have given themselves to Him includes,

- Jn 14:2–3: "In my Father's house are many mansions; if it were not so I would have told you. I go to prepare a place for you. And if I go and prepare a place for you I will come again, and receive you unto Myself; that where I am, there you may be also."
- 1Co 15:24, 28: "Then comes the end, when He delivers up the kingdom to God the Father, when He puts an end to all rule and authority and power … Now when all things are subject to Him, then the Son Himself will also be subject to Him Who put all things under Him, that God may be all in all."

If we have not given ourselves to Christ, we will remain on earth for judgment.

- Lk 17:34–36: "I tell you in that night there shall be two men in one bed; the one shall be taken, and the other shall be left. Two women shall be grinding together; the one shall be taken, and the other left. Two men shall be in the field; the one shall be taken and the other left."
- Christ told His disciples in Lk 13:24–27: "Strive to enter in at the straight [narrow] gate: for many, I say unto you, will seek to enter in [when He comes], and shall not be able, when once the Master of the House is risen up, and has shut the door, and you begin to stand without, and to knock at the door, saying, Lord, Lord, open for us;' and He shall answer and say unto you, 'I do not know you, where you are from, then you will begin to say, 'We ate and drank in Your presence, and You taught in our streets.' But He shall say, 'I tell you I do not know you, where you are from. Depart from Me, all you workers of iniquity.'"

Just as we can look at the New Testament as the fulfillment of the first coming of Christ, we can look at Revelation as the fulfillment of His second coming. That means that every verse in this book can be backed up by prophecy in the Bible. It is always a challenge with the life of Jesus to see the prophecies that were fulfilled and here again to challenge ourselves to see if we can see where God has left us with the hope of His coming to bring eternal peace on earth and goodwill toward everyone.

It is my understanding from reading Revelation 2–3 of the character of the churches that only the overcomers will be taken in the rapture. The question is whether we are walking in the Spirit and seeing things as Christ sees them or walking in the flesh and still under the influence of Satan.

Resurrections

There are a series of resurrections or raptures in Revelation.

- Resurrection of Jesus Christ to the throne (Rev 1)
- Resurrection of the Old and New Testament saints (Rev 4)
- Resurrection of the Gentiles or the great multitude of tribulation saints (Rev 7)

- Resurrection of the two witnesses (Rev 11)
- Resurrection of the nation of Israel (Rev 14)
- Resurrection at the great white throne judgment (Rev 20)

7. Revelation of the Seventy Weeks of Daniel

The time period for the tribulation was given in prophesy by Daniel. He was praying for God's people, the Israelites, who were in captivity. He prayed for three weeks until Gabriel came and gave him the hope of humanity from that date throughout all eternity. Daniel 9:20–27 reads,

> Now while I was speaking, praying, and confessing my sin and the sin of my people Israel, and presenting my supplication before the Lord my God for the holy mountain [city of Jerusalem] of my God, yes, while I was speaking in prayer, the man Gabriel, whom I had seen in the vision at the beginning, being caused to fly swiftly, reached me about the time of the evening offering. And he informed me, and talked with me, and said, "O Daniel, I have now come forth to give you skill to understand. At the beginning of your supplications the command went out, and I have come to tell you, for you are greatly beloved; therefore consider the matter, and understand the vision: Seventy weeks are determined For your people and for your holy city, To finish the transgression, To make an end of sins, To make reconciliation for iniquity, To bring in everlasting righteousness, To seal up vision and prophecy, And to anoint the Most Holy. Know therefore and understand, That from the going forth of the command To restore and build Jerusalem Until Messiah the Prince, There shall be seven weeks and sixty-two weeks; The street shall be built again, and the wall, Even in troublesome times. And after the sixty-two weeks Messiah shall be cut off, but not for Himself; And the people of the prince who is to come Shall destroy the city and the sanctuary. The end of it shall

be with a flood, And till the end of the war desolations are determined. Then he shall confirm a covenant with many for one week; But in the middle of the week He shall bring an end to sacrifice and offering. And on the wing of abominations shall be one who makes desolate, Even until the consummation, which is determined, Is poured out on the desolate."

Seventy Weeks of Daniel

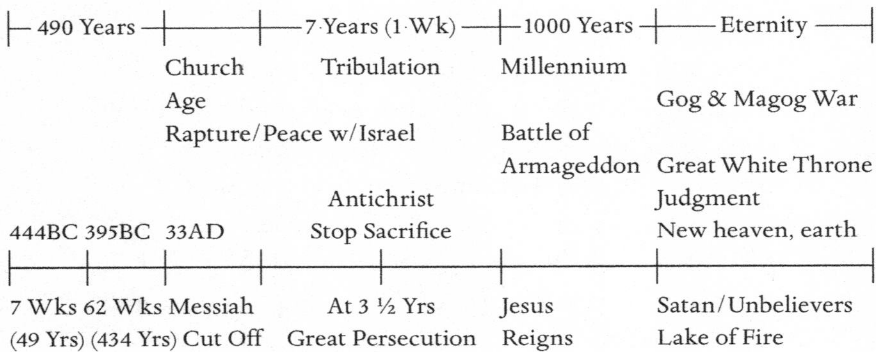

Here is the interpretation of Daniel 9:20–27 on the previous page. The seventy weeks of Daniel are the seven years of the tribulation.

- From the time of the release of the Israelites from captivity, Cyrus invited the Jews to rebuild the temple. It began in 444 BC and was completed in 395 BC (49 years).
- The sixty-two weeks are 434 years from that time to the time that Messiah was killed. The Messiah was cut off in AD 33.There is no time period given before the seventieth week (tribulation).
- The tribulation begins with two events that will happen at the same time: the church will be raptured, and the Antichrist will confirm a covenant with many (Israel) for one week (seven years). The temple in Israel will be rebuilt, and the Jews will reestablish their sacrifice and offering.

- In the middle of the week (three and a half years), the Antichrist will require Israel to worship him, and their eyes will be opened to the truth.
- On the wing of abominations shall be one who makes desolate until the consummation which is determined is poured out on the desolate. Those who do not wear the mark of the Beast (666) will be persecuted and face famine.
- At the end of the seven years, Christ will return (the second coming) for the Battle of Armageddon, and Christ will defeat the Antichrist and have him thrown into the bottomless pit so Christ can rule and reign on the earth for a thousand years.
- Satan will be released but still as the deceiver will lead a rebellion and convince one-third of the people to rebel as well. The satanic trinity will be cast into the lake of fire.
- The great white throne judgment will judge all people. Nonbelievers will join Satan in the lake of fire.
- New Jerusalem will come, and the earth will change. Jesus will have overcome Satan and all the evil he brought forth. God's plan for humanity will be complete.

Time Line for Book of Revelation

(# refers to chapter, * denotes resurrection)

Old Testament | Church | Tribulation | Millennium | Eternity
Age Mid Trib Armageddon Gog & Magog

-------------------|-----------|-------------|-------------|--------------------|----------------------

Chapters 1-11: Story of Jesus as Lord

* (1) Jesus' Resurrection to the Throne of God 2000 years ago

(2&3) Church Age with Jesus at the center of His Church; redeemed; received eternal life

* (4) Rapture of Old and New Testament Saints

(5) All heaven celebrates the kingdom has come; Jesus rolls out the scroll, His inheritance

(6) <u>Seal Judgments</u>; Antichrist treaty w/Israel: worship in Temple (1/4 people destroyed)

* (7) 144,000 (symbolizes all Israel) sealed; multitude resurrected

<u>(8) Silence; Trumpet Judgments (1/3 of creation is destroyed by God)</u>

(9) Locust Plague (5 months prior to mid trib – life span of locusts)

(10) No more delay

(11) Measure the Temple – Gentiles left will be trampled upon

* | 2 witnesses killed, resurrected in 3 days; earth quake, 7000 killed

Chapters 12-13: Story of Satan as Destroyer

(12:1) Woman Israel birthed 12 tribes (Gen 29-30)

(12:4) Satan thrown from heaven to earth; earth destroyed because Satan continued to sin (Ez 28:18)

(12:2) Satan has access to the Throne as accuser of the brethren (Job 1)

| (12:4) Jesus born; Satan always ready to devour

(12:5) Jesus snatched by God to Throne

| (13:5) War for 42 months or 3/1/2 years or 1260 days

Chapters 14-22: Lamb Rules the Kingdom

* (14:1) Lamb comes to Mt Zion to bring Israel to heaven

(14:4) Harvest (<u>Bowl Judgments</u>); announce kingdom to nations

(14:14-20) Reap Harvest

(15) Celebrate King Messiah

(16) Judgment poured upon earth and upon Beasts

(16:16) Antichrist prepares for Battle of Armageddon

(17) Announce destruction of Babylon; 7/heads/10 horns

(18) Announce one hour judgment

(19) Jesus/army of heaven on white horses; rule earth

(19:9) Marriage Supper of the Lamb

(19:17) No battle; Sword of the Lord

(19:20) Antichrist & False Prophet – Lake of Fire

(20:1) Satan bound 1000 years in bottomless pit

| Temple Worship |

(20:7) Satan released; Gog & Magog

* (20:11) Great White Throne Judgment

(20:10) Satan/Unbelievers /Lake of Fire

(21:1) New heaven, earth, etc.

Chronological Sequence of Revelation

Chapter 1: Revelation of Christ Resurrected	
Christ on His throne	1. Christ is on the throne of God (Rev 1:2) 2. Christ's message to His church (Rev 1:4) 3. Christ is King (Rev 1:5) 4. Christ is coming (Rev 1:7) 5. Christ is Lord (Rev 1:8) 6. Christ is High Priest (Rev 1:13) 7. Christ is Judge in the sevenfold glory of His person (Rev 1:14–20)
Chapters 2–3: Revelation of Christ's Church	
Each church represents a part of the whole of the church age.	1. Ephesus—backslidden church (AD 70–170) 2. Smyrna—persecuted church (AD 170–312) 3. Pergamos—wicked church (AD 312–606) 4. Thyatira—lax church (AD 606–1520) 5. Sardis—dead church (AD 1520–1750) 6. Philadelphia—favored church (AD 1750–1900) 7. Laodicea—lukewarm church (AD 1900–Rapture)
Chapters 4–5: Revelation of Christ Receiving His Inheritance	
Church is raptured.	1. The throne room of heaven (Rev 4:1) 2. First judgment—bema seat judgment of the church (Rev 4:2–3) 3. Five crowns (Rev 4:4–5a) 4. Seven spirits of God (Rev 4:5b) 5. Four living creatures (Rev 4:6–11) 6. The Lamb takes the scroll (Rev 5:1–7) 7. Worthy is the Lamb (Rev 5:8–14)

<table>
<tr><th colspan="2">Chapters 6–7: Revelation of the Seal Judgments</th></tr>
<tr><td>Seven seal judgments: God allows Antichrist to make a contract with Israel for peace. Antichrist will punish those (Hebrew and Gentile) who rejected the Godhead. Seven seal judgments comprise an overview of seven years.</td><td>1. White horse—Antichrist arrives as deceiver (Rev 6:2)
2. Red horse—Antichrist brings persecution (Rev 6:4)
3. Black horse—Antichrist brings worldwide famine (Rev 6:5)
4. Pale horse—Antichrist brings death to a quarter of the world population (Rev 6:8)
5. Antichrist brings martyrdom to those who will not worship him (Rev 6:9)
6. God brings cosmic disorders; people cry out to end the wrath (Rev 6:12)
7. God will seal His people (Rev 7:17)</td></tr>
<tr><th colspan="2">Chapters 8–11: Revelation of the Trumpet Judgments</th></tr>
<tr><td>God allows those who continue to reject Him and will not repent to be punished.</td><td>1. One-third of the vegetation and sea creatures will be destroyed (Rev 8:7)
2. One-third of the seas turn to blood; one-third of the people die of lack of water (Rev 8:8)
3. One-third of the fresh water rivers will become contaminated (Rev 8:10)
4. One-third of sun, moon, and stars are darkened; one-third day will not shine (Rev 8:12)
5. Demon locusts inflict those with the mark of the Beast five months (Rev 9:1)
6. One-third of humanity will be slayed by army of two hundred million (Rev 9:13)
7. Second Judgment (Jews)—Seven thunders announce the glory of the Kingdom of Christ (Rev 11:15)</td></tr>
</table>

Chapters 12–13: Revelation of the Great Tribulation (Characters)	
Antichrist is no longer the deceiver; he is thrown out of heaven.	1. The sun-clothed woman (Rev 12:1–2) 2. The dragon (Rev 12:3–4) 3. The Man-Child (Rev 12:5–6) 4. The archangel (Rev 12:7–12) 5. The Jewish remnant (Rev 12:13–17) 6. The beast out of the sea—political leader (Rev 13:1–10) 7. The beast out of the earth—religious leader (Rev 13:11–18)
Chapter 14–15 Revelation of Christ with the Tribulation Saints	
Seven angels proclaim the victory of King Jesus.	1. The 144,000 are sealed—Israel will be resurrected (Rev 14:1–7) 2. Babylon is fallen (Rev 14:8) 3. Torment to those who receive the mark (Rev 14:9–13) 4. Reap the harvest (Rev 14:14–16 5. Grapes are ripe (Rev 14:17–20) 6. Winepress is trampled (Rev 14:19–20) 7. God's temple in heaven is filled with glory (Rev 15:1–8)
Chapters 16: Revelation of the Bowl Judgments	
God will deliver his wrath on all those who wear the mark of the Beast.	1. All will be afflicted with foul sores (Rev 16:2) 2. All seas will be filled with blood; all sea creatures will die (Rev 16:3) 3. All rivers will be filled with blood for killing martyrs (Rev 16:4) 4. All those on the earth will be scorched by the sun (Rev 16:8) 5. All darkness and great pain will overcome them (Rev 16:10) 6. Euphrates River is dried up for Battle of Armageddon to occur (Rev 16:12) 7. Christ returns to earth for the second coming (Rev 16:17)

Chapter 17–19: Revelation of Christ's Victory over Babylon	
Christ returns for the Battle of Armageddon.	1. One-world religious system is destroyed (Rev 17:1–6) 2. One-world government and financial systems are destroyed (Rev 18:1–8) 3. Babylon's fall (Rev 18:21–24) 4. Heaven exults over Babylon (Rev 19:1–10) 5. Marriage supper of the Lamb (Rev 19:8–10) 6. Christ comes to Armageddon (Rev 19:11–16) 7. Antichrist and Antispirit are cast into the lake of fire (Rev 19:17–21)
Chapter 20: Revelation of the Millennial Rule by Christ	
Jesus will rule from His throne in a temple He will resurrect in Jerusalem.	1. Satan is judged 1,000 years (Rev 20:1–3) 2. Nations are judged (Rev 20:4a) 3. Resurrection of the dead (Rev 20:4b) 4. Christ reigns during the millennium (Rev 20:5–6) 5. Satan is loosed (Rev 20:7–8) 6. Satan is cast into the lake of fire (Rev 20:9) 7. All are judged—great white throne judgment (Rev 20:11–15)
Chapters 21–22: Revelation of New Things	
All things will be made new.	1. New Heaven (Rev 21:1) 2. New Earth (Rev 21:2–8) 3. New Jerusalem (Rev 21:9–23) 4. New Nations (Rev 21:24–27) 5. New River of Water of Life (Rev 22:1) 6. New Tree of Life (Rev 22:2) 7. New Throne (Rev 22:3–5)

CHAPTER 1

Revelation 1: Christ Resurrected

Jesus invites John the apostle to heaven to see a firsthand glimpse of Jesus resurrected to the throne of God. In this chapter, we see Jesus in the same roles as described in Hebrews: as King, Lord, High Priest, and Judge.

1. Christ is on the Throne of God (Rev 1:1–3)
2. Christ's Message is to His church (Rev 1:4)
3. Christ is King (Rev 1:5–6)
4. Christ is Coming—The Hope of Glory (Rev 1:7)
5. Christ is Lord (Rev 1:8–12)
6. Christ is High Priest (Rev 1:13)
7. Christ is Judge in the Sevenfold Glory of His Person (Rev 1:14–20)

1. Christ is on the Throne of God (Rev 1:1–2)

> *[1]The Revelation of Jesus Christ, which God gave Him to show His servants—things which must shortly take place. And He sent and signified it by His angel to His servant John, [2]who bore witness to the word of God, and to the testimony of Jesus Christ, to all things that he saw.*

Chapter 1 contains the "things which you have seen." Jesus is showing John proof that He is on the throne of God and that He died, was buried, and rose again in fulfillment of the Scriptures. Jesus had shown Himself to John when He was resurrected on earth but now wants him to have a "revelation" of what heaven looks like. After all, when Jesus went to hell,

He released those in paradise, the holding area for the Old Testament saints awaiting Jesus to forgive them their sins so they could enter to see the Father through Jesus Christ.

Since then, all our family members, those who trusted Jesus as their Savior, have gone directly to heaven to be with Jesus. John stated at the beginning in His gospel, again in his epistles, and now again at the end of the New Testament, that the deity of Christ was the truth of the Word of God. This is the revelation of Christ shown by His angel to John.

- Jn 1:1–2: "In the beginning was the Word, and the Word was with God, and the Word was God. He was in the beginning with God."
- Jn 3:32–33: "And what He has seen and heard, that He testifies; and no one receives His testimony. He who has received His testimony has certified that God is true."
- 1Jn 1:1–4: "That which was from the beginning, which we have heard, which we have seen with our eyes, which we have looked upon, and our hands have handled, concerning the Word of life—the life was manifested, and we have seen, and bear witness, and declare to you that eternal life which was with the Father and was manifested to us—that which we have seen and heard we declare to you, that you also may have fellowship with us; and truly our fellowship is with the Father and with His Son Jesus Christ. And these things we write to you that your joy may be full."
- Rev 22:6-7: "Then he said to me, 'These words are faithful and true.' And the Lord God of the holy prophets sent His angel to show His servants the things which must shortly take place. Behold, I am coming quickly! Blessed is he who keeps the words of the prophecy of this book."
- 1Co 1:4–8: Paul confirmed this, "I thank my God always concerning you for the grace of God which was given to you by Christ Jesus, that you were enriched in everything by Him in all utterance and all knowledge, even as the testimony of Christ was confirmed in you, so that you come short in no gift, eagerly waiting for the revelation of our Lord Jesus Christ, who will also confirm you to the end, that you may be blameless in the day of our Lord Jesus Christ."

The Greek phrase "shortly come to pass" *(en takhei)* does not mean soon, but when it happens, it will come quickly and the judgments will be in rapid succession. "Signified" means signs and symbols:

> [3]*Blessed is he who reads and those who hear the words of this prophecy, and keep those things which are written in it; for the time is near.*

Jesus begins by blessing His followers, those who keep this message in their heart.

- Lk 11:8: Luke confirmed that we will receive all blessings promised by God, "I say to you, though he will not rise and give to him because he is his friend, yet because of his persistence he will rise and give him as many as he needs."
- Jas 5:8: James confirmed the truth of God's Word, "You also be patient. Establish your hearts, for the coming of the Christ is at hand."

2. Christ's Message is to His Church (Rev 1:4)

> [4a]*John, to the seven churches which are in Asia:*

Jesus asked John to write to the seven churches in Asia. They are a symbol of the whole church, because in chronological order, chapters 2 and 3 are the church age from the time Christ was resurrected until chapter 4, when He returns for the church. In Matthew 24, the disciples are asking when Christ will return for His followers. Matthew 24:13-14 says, "But he who shall endure unto the end shall be saved. And this Gospel of the kingdom shall be preached in all the world for a witness unto all nations and then shall the end come."

Revelation 1:11–13 refers to the seven churches as seven golden candlesticks, which are a symbol for the church. Then in Revelation 4:5, these seven lamps are before the throne, which indicates the rapture of the church.

John was in awe. The message of Revelation is to the church, which is told to look for Jesus to come; the rapture is the hope of the church when all things will be consummated.

> [4b]*Grace to you and peace from Him who is and who was and who is to come, and from the seven Spirits who are before His throne ...*

Grace and peace came by the sacrifice of Jesus on the cross. The seven spirits before His throne are the fullness of the Holy Spirit of Christ (Isa 11:2). These seven spirits describe the character of the Holy Spirit. They are the spirits that the Holy Spirit manifests in believers.

1. The spirit of the Lord is the ability to have the same nature as Jesus.
2. The spirit of wisdom is the ability to walk in righteousness.
3. The spirit of understanding is the ability to have God's understanding in everything.
4. The spirit of counsel is the ability to surrender to the Holy Spirit's guidance.
5. The spirit of might is the ability to perform God's Word.
6. The spirit of knowledge is the ability to know how to walk in the spirit and not in the flesh.
7. The spirit of the fear of the Lord is the ability to respect God's presence.

3. Christ is King (Rev 1:5–6)

> [5]*and from Jesus Christ, the faithful witness, the firstborn from the dead, and the ruler over the kings of the earth. To Him who loved us and washed us from our sins in His own blood,* [6]*and has made us kings and priests to His God and Father, to Him be glory and dominion forever and ever. Amen.*

The message is from our King, our Messiah, Jesus Christ, who was the only one who was obedient to be faithful to redeem the church. He loved us so much that He sacrificed Himself to be our Savior. Jesus Christ is the firstborn of all heirs (the church). Heirs are kings and priests of God who give glory for their earthly dominion today. Christ's sacrifice set apart believers as the priesthood who sacrifice.

- 1Pe 2:9–10: "But you are a chosen generation, a royal priesthood, a holy nation, His own special people, that you may proclaim the praises of Him Who called you out of darkness into His marvelous light; who once were not a people but are now the people of God, who had not obtained mercy but now have obtained mercy."
- Ex 3:14: "And God said to Moses, 'I AM WHO I AM.' And He said, 'Thus you shall say to the children of Israel, "I AM has sent me to you."'"
- 1Ti 6:13–16: "I urge you in the sight of God Who gives life to all things, and before Christ Jesus Who witnessed the good confession before Pontius Pilate, that you keep this commandment without spot, blameless until our Lord Jesus Christ's appearing, which He will manifest in His own time, He Who is the blessed and only Potentate, the King of kings and Lord of lords, Who alone has immortality, dwelling in unapproachable light, Whom no man has seen or can see, to Whom be honor and everlasting power. Amen."

4. Christ is Coming—The Hope of Glory (Rev 1:7)

> *[7]Behold, He is coming with clouds, and every eye will see Him, even they who pierced Him. And all the tribes of the earth will mourn because of Him. Even so. Amen.*

Christ is coming as King of Kings. He will catch the church in the air (rapture) and return in the same manner as He went up—in a cloud. (This is covered in chapter 4.) The Jews will know that Jesus is their Messiah. They will mourn because they will have to go through the tribulation because they did not believe through faith in the Son of God.

- Mt 24:30: "Then the sign of the Son of Man will appear in heaven, and then all the tribes of the earth will mourn, and they will see the Son of Man coming on the clouds of heaven with power and great glory."

- 1Th 4:16–17: "For the Lord himself shall descend from heaven with a shout, with the voice of the archangel, and with the trump of God: and the dead in Christ shall rise first: Then we which are alive and remain shall be caught up together with them in the clouds, to meet the Lord in the air: and so shall we ever be with the Lord."

The dead in Christ will rise first, and then those alive will be caught up together. Their soul and spirit will enter their resurrected body that is to become their glorified body.

- 1Co 15:51–52: "Behold, I tell you a mystery: We shall not all sleep, but we shall all be changed—in a moment, in the twinkling of an eye, at the last trumpet. For the trumpet will sound, and the dead will be raised incorruptible, and we shall be changed."
- Jn 5:24: "Most assuredly, I say unto you, he that hears My word and believes in Him who sent Me has everlasting life, and shall not come into judgment; but has passed from death unto life."

There are no specific prophecies that have to be fulfilled before the rapture occurs. They have all been fulfilled.

- 1Th 5:2: "For you yourselves know perfectly that the day of the Lord so comes as a thief in the night."

The church is also called the bride of Christ, which will be brought to the Father. Revelation is a picture of the ancient Jewish wedding. There are four stages:

1. The bride is approved by the Father.

    - 2Co 11:2: "For I am jealous for you with Godly jealousy. For I have betrothed you to one husband, that I may present you as a chaste virgin to Christ."

- Ro 7:4: "Therefore, my brethren, you also have become dead to the law through the body of Christ, that you may be married to another—to Him who was raised from the dead, that we should bear fruit to God."
- Jn 15:16: "You did not choose Me, but I chose you and appointed you that you should go and bear fruit, and that your fruit should remain, that whatever you ask the Father in My name He may give you."
- Eph 1:11–12: "In Him also we have obtained an inheritance, being predestined according to the purpose of Him who works all things according to the counsel of His will, that we who first trusted in Christ should be to the praise of His glory."

2. The bride is stolen away and taken to the Father's house (the rapture).

    - Jn 14:3: "And if I go and prepare a place for you, I will come again and receive you to Myself; that where I am, there you may be also."

3. The couple spends a week together in the room. While the festivities go on, a gala event is had by the guests during that time (a week is as a year). The seven-year tribulation is depicted here.

4. They get to know each other spiritually. Then they join those who have come to celebrate the marriage. Christ will spend seven years in heaven with His bride preparing her for the millennium. After the celebration comes the marriage supper of the lamb after which depart to earth to rule and reign together during one-thousand years or the millennium.

5. Christ is Lord (Rev 1:8–12)

> *8 "I am the Alpha and the Omega, the Beginning and the End," says the Lord, "Who is and Who was and Who is to come, the Almighty."*

Christ is the Alpha and Omega, the first and last letters of the Greek alphabet. It means sovereignty, that He always was the Creator and sustainer of the universe (Alpha) and will live for eternity (Omega). Jesus is the Lord of the Bible, throughout the Old and New Testaments—Almighty is His name Who was and is and will be for eternity.

- Is 9:6: "For unto us a Child is born, unto us a Son is given; and the government will be upon His shoulder. And His name will be called Wonderful, Counselor, Mighty God, Everlasting Father, Prince of Peace."
- Is 41:4: "Who has performed and done it, calling the generations from the beginning? 'I, the Lord, *am* the first; and with the last I *am* He.'"

> [9]*I, John, both your brother and companion in the tribulation and kingdom and patience of Jesus Christ, was on the island that is called Patmos for the word of God and for the testimony of Jesus Christ.* [10]*I was in the Spirit on the Lord's Day, and I heard behind me a loud voice, as of a trumpet,* [11]*saying, "I am the Alpha and the Omega, the First and the Last," and, "What you see, write in a book and send it to the seven churches which are in Asia: to Ephesus, to Smyrna, to Pergamos, to Thyatira, to Sardis, to Philadelphia, and to Laodicea."* [12] *Then I turned to see the voice that spoke with me. And having turned I saw seven golden lampstands.*

John was Jesus' companion who wrote Revelation on Patmos where he was banished because He stood for Christ. It was Sunday, the Lord's Day. Here, we see the lampstands are the seven spiritual symbols or characteristics, the spiritual image of the church.

- Ex 25:37: Moses ordered the making of the Golden lampstand to be placed in the Holy of Holies, "You shall make seven lamps for it, and they shall arrange its lamps so that they give light in front of it."
- Ex 37:23: "And he made its seven lamps, its wick-trimmers, and its trays of pure gold."

6. Christ Is High Priest (Rev 1:13)

> *[13]and in the midst of the seven lampstands One like the Son of Man, clothed with a garment down to the feet and girded about the chest with a golden band.*

This is a picture of Christ, the Son of Man (Jesus), and now is in this dispensation in the midst of His people. He is clothed with a garment to His feet, girded with a golden band. This describes Jesus Christ as our High Priest, our Intercessor, and our Mediator today.

- Ex 28:4: "And these are the garments which they shall make: a breastplate, an ephod, a robe, a skillfully woven tunic, a turban, and a sash. So they shall make holy garments for Aaron your brother and his sons, that he may minister to Me as priest."

7. Christ is Judge in the Sevenfold Glory of His Person (Rev 1:14–20)

In the Bible, descriptions are usually of the spiritual nature. One of the most important verses is Genesis 1:26, when God says, "Let us make man in our image." God is a spirit and sees us spiritually. Our relationship is spirit to spirit. Our spirit is commanded in verse 1:28 to "Be fruitful and multiply." Multiply what? Multiply God's spirit on earth. If we want to know our mandate, God placed it in the first chapter of His book. Here is a spiritual picture of Christ on the throne; His character is His spiritual image.

1. His Head and His Hair

> *[14a]His head and hair were white like wool, as white as snow,*

He is the Ancient of Days as described in Daniel 7:9; His hair was like pure wool, a symbol. The Ancient of Days is God as Judge in the universal court in heaven. Jesus Christ took on the role of the Judge, the Ancient of Days, seated on the throne of God. His head is white as snow, which symbolizes purity, holiness, majesty, and authority.

- Da 7:9–10: "I watched till Thrones were put in place, and the Ancient of Days was seated; His garment was white as snow, and the hair of His head was like pure wool. His Throne was a fiery flame; its wheels burning fire; a fiery stream issued and came forth from before Him. A thousand thousands ministered to Him; ten thousand times ten thousand stood before Him. The court was seated, and the books were opened."
- Da 10:6: "His body was like beryl, His face like the appearance of lightning, His eyes like torches of fire, His arms and feet like burnished bronze in color, and the sound of His words like the voice of a multitude."

2. His Eyes

> 14b *and His eyes like a flame of fire;*

Daniel 7:9 above says His throne was a fiery flame from which He will always judge in righteousness.

3. His Feet

> 15 *His feet were like fine brass, as if refined in a furnace.*

His feet are fine brass as if refined in a furnace; the refiner's fire takes our humanity and makes us pure.

- Ez 1:7: "Their legs were straight, and the soles of their feet were like the soles of calves' feet. They sparkled like the color of burnished bronze."

4. His Voice

> 15b *and His voice as the sound of many waters;*

His voice is that of living water; the Holy Spirit is the powerful manifestation of Christ. This is the voice of Jesus as the Judge. This voice will command all twenty-one of the judgments to be poured out by His angels during the tribulation.

- Ez 1:24: "When they went, I heard the noise of their wings, like the noise of many waters, like the voice of the Almighty, a tumult like the noise of an army; and when they stood still, they let down their wings."
- Ez 43:2: "And behold, the glory of the God of Israel came from the way of the east. His voice was like the sound of many waters; and the earth shone with His glory."

5. His Hand

> [16a] *He had in His right hand seven stars,*

The seven stars in His right hand (power and authority) represent the pastors in the church.

- Rev 1:20: "The seven stars are the angels of the seven churches, and the seven lampstands which you saw are the seven churches."

6. His Mouth

> [16b] *out of His mouth went a sharp two-edged sword,*

The two-edged sword judges with the power of the Word of God (Heb 1:3).

- Is 49:2: "And He has made My mouth like a sharp sword; in the shadow of His hand He has hidden Me, and made Me a polished shaft; in His quiver He has hidden Me."
- Heb 4:12: "For the word of God is living and powerful, and sharper than any two-edged sword, piercing even to the division of soul and spirit, and of joints and marrow, and is a discerner of the thoughts and intents of the heart."

7. His Countenance

> [16c]*and His countenance was like the sun shining in its strength.*

His countenance was like sun shining in His glory, and its strength was that Jesus overcame Satan when He was resurrected.

> [17]*And when I saw Him, I fell at His feet as dead. But He laid His right hand on me, saying to me, "Do not be afraid; I am the First and the Last.* [18]*I am He who lives, and was dead, and behold, I am alive forevermore. Amen. And I have the keys of Hades and of Death."*

John fell at His feet as dead as the man in Mark 9:26 after he was with Jesus. After someone saw Christ in person or the angel of the Lord, he or she must be in awe of His glory. There are sixty-five Bible verses that say, "Do not be afraid." Jesus is the first and the last; He has the keys to hell—the world as we knew it has changed, and there is nothing to fear.

- Is 41:4: "Who has performed and done it, calling the generations from the beginning? 'I, the Lord, *am* the first; and with the last I *am* He.'"
- Is 44:6: "Thus says the Lord, the King of Israel, and his Redeemer, the Lord of hosts: I *am* the First and I *am* the Last; besides Me there is no God."
- Is 48:12: "Listen to Me, O Jacob, and Israel, My called: I *am* He, I *am* the First, I *am* also the Last."
- Ez 1:28: "Like the appearance of a rainbow in a cloud on a rainy day, so was the appearance of the brightness all around it. This was the appearance of the likeness of the glory of the Lord. So when I saw it, I fell on my face, and I heard a voice of One speaking."

> [19]*Write the things which you have seen, and the things which are, and the things which will take place after this.* [20] *The mystery of the seven stars which you saw in My right hand, and*

the seven golden lampstands: The seven stars are the angels of the seven churches, and the seven lampstands which you saw are the seven churches.

The mystery of the seven stars is the angels or ministers of the seven lampstands, which are the church.

CHAPTER 2

Revelation 2–3: Christ's Church

There are two parts to this section. First, we will go through the church age, and then cover chapters 2 and 3 of what Christ reveals of the character of those churches.

Part One—The Church Age

Rulership	Church	Condition	Time	Church Period
Roman Empire (Nero)	Ephesus	Backslidden	70–170	Apostolic Church
Roman Empire (Hadrian)	Smyrna	Persecuted	170–312	Ecumenical Church
Byzantine Empire	Pergamos	Wicked	312–606	Christian Church
Crusades (Dark Ages)	Thyatira	Lax	606–1520	Dark Ages Church
Ottoman Empire (Greece)	Sardis	Dead	1520–1750	Reformed Church
Revivalism	Philadelphia	Favored	1750–1900	Enlightened Church
Modernism	Laodicea	Lukewarm	1900–rapture	Apostate Church

Looking at Revelation from a chronological standpoint, between chapter 1 (Christ's resurrection) and chapter 4 (rapture of the church), we find chapters 2–3 (church age). Many commentaries see the seven churches chronologically through the church age.

Ephesus, the Apostolic Church (70–170)—Backslidden Church

The apostolic period began with the birth of the church on the day of Pentecost. There was a great proliferation of heresy in the church. Gnosticism (head knowledge) was to deny Jesus' death, that He had not come in the flesh, and that there was no incarnation.

The original church was the true, universal body of Christ known as the apostolic church. The apostles devoted themselves to teaching, fellowship, breaking of bread, and prayer. Every day, they met in the temple courts. Even though they had a mega church, they had intimacy as hundreds of home meetings were held. The apostolic belief was that God raised Jesus Christ, His Son, from the dead. God has only children, no grandchildren, and therefore, each believer has to be a follower of Christ to be "born again" into the family of God.

Paul expanded the church from the center in Jerusalem when he created another mother church in Antioch, Asia Minor, and then a third in Ephesus.

All of the apostles were martyred.

- Andrew was tied to a cross, yet he preached till the end.
- Barnabas was stoned to death.
- James, the brother of John, was beheaded in Jerusalem.
- The second James was tossed from the temple to his death.
- John escaped death when he was boiled in oil. He was exiled to Patmos to die a normal death.
- Jude was a target for arrows until his death.
- Mark was dragged through the city of Alexandria to his death.
- Matthias was stoned and then beheaded.
- Paul was beheaded in Rome.
- Peter was crucified upside down at Rome when he refused the same crucifixion as his Lord.
- Thomas was killed with a sword.

Nero had Jerusalem and the temple destroyed in AD 70. Because the early believers came declaring that there was another king, Jesus, it did not take long for the church to be viewed as a serious threat in the emperor-worshiping Roman Empire. Christians and Hebrews continued to be persecuted and martyred. During Nero's attacks, a million Hebrews were murdered at the hands of the unrelenting Roman legions. When Nero burned Rome, he shifted the blame on Christians. Jews took strong action against Christians, and the synagogues became closed to Christian evangelism.

The gospel message was passed on from one disciple to another. Bally[2] wrote that the apostles were martyred with the influx of hatred toward Christians and gave this account:

- "Barnabas followed Paul and wrote, 'In six thousand years the Lord God will bring all things to an end.'
- Clement of Rome followed Peter and Paul.
- Polycarp, Bishop of Smyrna, followed John. Polycarp was asked to renounce Christ and wrote, 'Eighty-six years have I served Him, and He has done me no wrong; how then can I blaspheme my Savior and King?' In AD 155, he was burned at the stake.
- Ignatius, the bishop of Antioch, wrote, 'Let the laity be subject to the deacons; the deacons to the presbyters; the presbyters to the bishop; the bishop to Christ, even as He is to the Father.' In AD 115, he was thrown to the wild beasts in the Coliseum.
- Justin Martyr, in his *First Apology*, wrote, 'Others heal the sick by laying their hands upon them, and they are made whole … the dead even have been raised up, and remained among us for many years … we do also hear many brethren in the Church who possess prophetic gifts and who through the Spirit speak all kinds of languages.' In AD 165, he was beheaded.
- Iranaeus, bishop of Lyons in Gaul, was a third-generation disciple of Polycarp. In his book *Proof of the Apostolic Preaching*, he wrote, 'For in as many days as this world was made, in so many thousand years shall it be concluded.'

- Novatian recognized the Holy Spirit when he wrote, 'The Holy Spirit … directs tongues, gives powers and healings, does wonderful works.'
- Tertullian's *Apology* gave commentary on the Lord's Prayer, baptism, and the Trinity."

The Ephesus church is seen as the backslidden church because of the teachings of Paul in the New Testament. Galatians 1:6–7 says, "I marvel that you are turning away so soon from Him Who called you in the grace of Christ, to a different Gospel, which is not another; but there are some who trouble you and want to pervert the Gospel of Christ."

When Paul traveled on, the Judaizers would come in after him and teach that in order to be a Christian, you had to be circumcised; you had to remain a Jew because Jesus was a Jew. Paul wrote in 1 Corinthians 1:10–11, "Now I plead with you, brethren, by the name of our Lord Jesus Christ, that you all speak the same thing, and that there be no divisions among you, but that you be perfectly joined together in the same mind and in the same judgment. For it has been declared to me concerning you, my brethren, by those of Chloe's household, that there are contentions among you."

The writings of Paul were to explain the truth to the newly established church that was falling away.

Smyrna, the Ecumenical Church (170–312)—Persecuted Church

The Roman Empire continued in power, persecuting Christians.

- AD 135: Emperor Hadrian changed the name of the territory from Canaan to Palestine.
- AD 161–180: Emperor Marcus Aurelius thoroughly disliked Christians and had Bishop Telesphorus of Rome executed as well as Christians in Gaul (later France) and Africa.
- AD 249–251: Decius was the most violent emperor to persecute the church and commanded all citizens to sacrifice to the traditional Roman gods. Those who refused were executed.

- AD 251–253: Emperor Gallienus followed Decius's anti-Christian measures.
- AD 253–260: Emperor Valerian forbad church meetings or to visit Christian cemeteries.
- AD 284–305: Emperor Diocletian issued edicts to destroy all church buildings, confiscate Christian books, dismiss Christians from the government and army, and imprison the clergy. He then ordered all Christians to offer sacrifices to pagan gods, and all who did not were martyred.

Pergamos, the Christian Church (312–606)—Wicked Church

In AD 312, Emperor Constantine had a vision of a flaming cross and the words "By this sign conquer." He granted amnesty to all Christians, and they were accepted as the one main hope for unity and stability in the Roman Empire. Constantine called an ecumenical council to form doctrine and establish the Nicene Creed as the foundation of Christianity.

While Constantine meant well when he issued a decree that all his subjects should become Christians, it actually did much damage to the church. The majority of people became Christian in name only, bringing their pagan practices and lifestyles into a compromised church. This also fostered an anti-Semitic attitude as Jews were forced to give up all ties to Judaism and Jewish practices.

Constantine moved the capital of his empire to Byzantium, modern-day Istanbul, and renamed it Constantinople after himself.

Five Changes in the Church

1. The Apostle's Creed defined the Christian faith.
2. The canon of apostolic writing consisted of twelve apostolic statements of faith.
3. The position of bishop was introduced.
4. The Church of Rome rose in supremacy.
5. The gospel message was defined.

Jerome (AD 345–420), a biblical scholar, referred to the Old Testament (the Septuagint) and the Greek New Testament to prepare the fresh Latin translation. He then translated the Old Testament based on the original Hebrew rather than the Greek. After twenty-three years, Jerome completed the Vulgate Bible, which was eventually accepted as the authorized Latin version for the Western church. It was reaffirmed by the Council of Trent in 1546.

In 570, Muhammad of Mecca in Arabia started a new religion, Islam. The Jews did not believe Muhammad could be their Messiah because he was not of the family of David. Muslim forces massacred more than a thousand Jews, sold their women and children into slavery, and divided their property. Muhammad received one-fifth of all spoils.

As Muhammad received more instructions from Allah, he enacted Surah 2:256 to "Let there be no compulsion in religion" and Surah 9:5 to "Kill those who join other gods." With his dictatorship to convert to Islam or death, Islam developed into a major Arabian power stretching across three continents.

In 632, Muhammad died and was succeeded by Abu Bakr as the first caliph. Under his leadership over the next ten years, the Arabs conquered Syria and Iraq, followed by Egypt, then Persia (Iran). They believed the charge was given to them by Allah through his prophet, Muhammad.

In 638, Arab armies conquered Palestine and moved into the Holy Land; they were in full control.

In 656, the official version of the Qu'ran, their holy scriptures, was established during the reign of Uthman, eighteen years after Muhammad's death. There was a civil war within Islam among the descendants of Muhammad and disputes of all kinds about who was the legitimate, appointed heir to the faith.

By 685, Shi'ite extremism in Iraq was part of this revolution. These root disputations persist to the present day—Islam was divided into Shiites and Sunni Muslims. The Shiites stayed with the caliph in Arabia, while the Sunnis became the African American Islamic community led by the Black Muslim, Louis Farrakhan.

In 691, Caliph Abd el-Malik commissioned the best architects to build the Dome of the Rock, believed to be built over the place where the Jewish temple was destroyed.

Thyatira, the Dark Ages Church (606–1520)—Lax Church

The Dark Ages of the church began in the sixth century, when famine and plague swept across the land. It was also the time of the crusaders, who demonstrated the deepening lack of spirituality of the church. Indulgences were sold whereby people could pay money to supposedly have their sins removed.

The Roman papacy was established, and the title bishop became pope. The medieval church, prior to the early reformers, affirmed the priesthood of all believers but did little to facilitate their reinstatement into ministry.

- Peter Waldo sought to imitate Christ, selling everything and going out to preach in the country. Though he was excommunicated, he preached against the corruption in the church and insisted that women and laymen could preach.
- John Wycliff maintained that salvation does not depend on a connection with the visible church or upon the mediation of the priesthood but solely on election by God. He condemned the worship of saints, relics, and pilgrimages. He translated the Bible from the Vulgate into the English vernacular.
- John Hus held that Christ, not Peter, was the head of the church and that the Bible was the sole rule for life.
- Erasmus regarded himself as a layman and supported himself with his publications, insisting that there could be no intermediaries between Christians and the Scriptures.

The crusades were battles between the Christians (descendants of Isaac) and the Muslims (descendants of Ishmael) to take possession of Jerusalem. They began in the eleventh century and ended in the thirteenth century.

First Crusade	1099	Crusaders slaughtered inhabitants and took Jerusalem from Muslims.
Second Crusade	1147	Jerusalem surrendered to Muslims.

Third Crusade	1189	England and France rescued and captured Christians only, no land.
Fourth Crusade	1198	Pope gained Constantinople and destroyed Muslim army.
Children's Crusade	1212	Thousands of children from France and Germany were slaughtered by Muslims.
Fifth Crusade	1217	Captured Demit, Egypt, by using the Nile as their gateway.
Sixth Crusade	1228	Summit whereby agreement for Christians to obtain Jerusalem and other holy cities. But in 1244, Muslims attacked Jerusalem and pushed out the crusaders.
Seventh Crusade	1277	Muslims overtook Jerusalem.

Europe was struck with the bubonic plague in 1347; it killed a third of the inhabitants. The Muslims became a political threat and began to advance into Europe. Muhammad II gained control of Constantinople in 1453. The Muslims under Egyptian Mamluks captured Jerusalem in 1516 and allowed Jews to live within the walls of Jerusalem and visit the Western Wall. In 1517, Ottoman Turkish Muslims ruled under Suleiman who recognized the right of Jews to the Western Wall and designated it as the Jews' place of worship.

Sardis, the Reformed Church (1520–1750)—Dead Church

By the fifteenth century, the church appeared dead; it took the reformation to bring it back to life. This was a time when the church had a reputation for being alive, but as God saw it, they were really dying. History revealed that though the churches of the reformation broke away from problems in the Roman Catholic Church, they still did not return to thoroughly biblical practices.

- Reformation Day was October 31, 1517, when Martin Luther, a Catholic monk and professor of Biblical Studies at the University of Wittenberg, Germany, nailed his *Ninety-Five Theses* to the door of the castle church in Wittenberg. This reformation was a breaking away from the Catholic Church to a Protestant faith. Luther declared that the church received salvation through faith alone. These are documented both in the Old and New Testaments (Hab 2:4 and Ro 1:17) that "the just shall live by faith." People had no great fear of hell because they believed that if they died, they could buy forgiveness and be blessed by a priest and guaranteed heaven.

Tetzel was a Dominican monk who sold indulgences to buy entrance into heaven and free a soul from purgatory. Luther said it encouraged sin and turned people away from Christ and God's forgiveness. Martin Luther called this "heresy" and taught that all doctrine in the church had to have its roots in the Bible. The Reformation was primarily a rediscovery of the gospel of God's saving work in Christ.

- In 1522, the Reformation church was established in Zurich, Switzerland, by Ulrich Zwingli. The Reformers believed in direct relation and union with Christ as the one, only, and all-sufficient source of grace by the power of the Holy Spirit through the Word of God.

- In the 1530s, the Anabaptists (later known as Mennonites) elaborated on congregational church authority where all members who were baptized voluntarily as adults were to be believers. Decision making was to be by the entire membership. Scripture was to be interpreted by consensus of the gathering. Both Protestants and Catholics felt threatened and joined to persecute thousands of Anti-Baptists. Not until the late nineteenth century did they experience revival, and by 1988, their worldwide membership had grown to 750,000.

- In 1536, John Calvin, following Luther's theology, was an exiled Frenchman who developed the Presbyterian Church government in which all church ministers served at the same level and the people were represented by lay elders. In that same year, he published the first edition of *The Institution of the Christian Religion*, giving clear defense of the Reformation beliefs.

Calvin set out the way of repentance, faith and sanctification. Calvin wrote: "Justification by faith is he who, excluded from the righteousness of works, grasps the righteousness of Christ through faith, and clothed in it, appears in God's sight not as a sinner but as a righteous man" (Institute 3.11).

- Jacobus Arminius was opposed to Calvinism. Arminianism reappeared in full vitality as the fiber of Wesleyan Methodism a century later. Arminianism advocated the following:

    - conditional election—God elects people on the basis of His foreknowledge of their choices
    - unlimited atonement—Christ died for all people
    - cooperation of the human will with divine grace
    - resistible grace
    - conditional security—the possibility of falling from grace

- In 1540, Ignatius of Loyola founded the Jesuits (the Society of Jesus); Jesuits vowed total obedience to the pope and published the *Spiritual Exercises* which all Roman Catholic ordainds had to go through. By 1556, the Jesuit society grew to 1,500 followers. By 1964, there were 36,038. Today, the Jesuits run about 4,000 schools, including nineteen universities in the United States.

- In 1560, John Knox studied Calvinism and launched the Reformation in Scotland, attacking the papacy, the Mass, and Catholic idolatry. Catholic Mary Queen of Scots opposed Knox. In 1560, Knox wrote his treatise on predestination. By 1587, the queen was eventually beaten and executed. Under King James I, many Presbyterian Scots settled in Northern Ireland.

- The Thirty-Year War lasted from 1618 until 1648 between Protestants and Catholics when Calvinism was not recognized as a legal religion. This politically, economically, and physically devastated Germany. At the Ecumenical Council of Trent, both Protestants and Catholics met. The Catholics upheld their original seven sacraments, the celibacy of the clergy, and the existence of purgatory. All hopes of Protestants restoring unity were destroyed.

- By 1626, the Puritan Pilgrims (Calvinists, Presbyterian, Anglicans, Lutherans, and Mennonites) migrated to America, and the first Baptist congregation grew from the separation of John Smythe. By 1660, there were roughly 300 Baptist churches. Queen Elizabeth established Protestantism in England and Ireland. She gradually replaced Catholic Church leaders with Protestants.

- George Fox was raised as a Presbyterian, trained in the Puritan religion, and was influenced early in life by the Anabaptists. His ministry was charismatic in nature. His followers would come together to wait upon the Spirit, and as they prayed, the power of God came down in such a marvelous manner that the very building seemed to rock or quake (Quakers).

  In 1652, the first Quaker community was formed, and in four years, Fox had fifty-six associate itinerant preachers with him. By 1660, the Quakers moved into the Western world and had over 50,000 adherents. There were more than 4,000 dissenting Quakers in English prisons.

- In the seventeenth century, Saxony count Nicolaus Ludwig von Zinzendorf was raised a Pietist whose whole life was Jesus and Jesus alone. He opened his castle to Moravian and Bohemian Protestants, and the revival movement lasted continually for one century. The Moravian Brethren were characterized by three qualities: a passionate zeal for the Lord, nondenominational barriers, and foreign missions. They even sold themselves as slaves for converts in the Caribbean.

Philadelphia, the Revivalism (1750–1900)—Enlightened Church

When the pilgrims came to the United States, the constitution was signed in 1776, placing the country one nation under God. The enlightenment period covered the missionary revivals of John Wesley, George Whitefield, Charles G. Finney, D. L. Moody, and C. H. Spurgeon, bringing forth love that caused the desire to evangelize others (Ro 5:5). Philadelphia is the church that means brotherly love.

- In 1727, the fire of Pentecost fell upon a church belonging to the United Brethren in Germany. They were devoted to meeting every evening to read the Bible and pray. In 1734, when the Dutch East India Company was dispatched to form a colony in America, John Wesley was converted crossing the Atlantic when through outrageous storms, the Moravians continued to sing and praise the Lord. John Wesley wanted to know how to have that faith and was told to preach savings grace until he received it.

  In 1738, John Wesley and George Whitefield started open-air preaching, which was the work of the Holy Spirit. Methodism stood as a strong spiritual force on both sides of the Atlantic in the ongoing recovery of the manifest presence of God upon the earth in the eighteenth century. George Whitefield went on to Scotland and to John Balfour's revival where the Holy Spirit continued to work. The Methodists drew up a common set of rules for their society, a group of people coming together to help each other work out their salvation. For the next twenty years, John Wesley supervised the Methodist Society in Bristol, England.

- In 1845, Charles Finney, an evangelist, fought for abolition of slavery, and the Southern Methodists declared themselves independent. During the American Civil War, chaplains received $100 a month from Congress to visit the fields and hospitals on both sides and to pray for victory.

- During the late 1800s, C. H. Spurgeon erected the Metropolitan Tabernacle, which seated 6,000. It was also a college that trained

900 pastors before Spurgeon's death. The college distributed literature, published a magazine entitled *The Sword and the Trowel*, and ran an orphanage.

- D. L. Moody was a dynamic evangelist in the late 1800s who founded the Chicago Evangelization Society, later known as the Moody Bible Institute.

Laodicea, the Apostate Church (1900–Rapture)—Lukewarm Church

The Enlightened Church of Philadelphia will increase until the rapture. In contrast, the last church period will also continue until the rapture. The Laodicea church means "rule of the people." It is a picture of a church controlled by the people instead of by God. It is the church of the apostasy, the great "falling away" of believers. To this church, Jesus says, "Behold, I stand at the door and knock. If anyone hears My voice and opens the door, I will come in to him and dine with him, and he with Me." (Rev 3:20) This is a church full of unsaved people. Since it comes at the end of the church age, it is easy to see that there will still be many who call themselves Christians left behind when the rapture takes place.

The new age, legalism, or modernism has crept in. Any religion not based on Jesus Christ as the Son of God is a false religion according to the Bible. The Bible that was dictated by God is believed to be the only one true doctrine. Satan is still the deceiver.

Part Two: The Churches of Revelation

In each church described in Revelation, a condition is stated, their sin, how to turn from that sin, and a promise if they turn to glorify God. Since this is a chronological study, we will look at each church accordingly. We must realize that each church described is seen in the characteristics of many of the churches today. It is certainly written for us today as a warning so we will conform to the righteousness of Christ, repent, and be overcomers so the promises of God as indicated in each church will be seen in our church and in each one of us.

Church	Condition	Sin	Warning/ Work	Promise/ Individual Reward
Ephesus (backslidden church 70–170)	Hate evil, patient, persevere	Left first love, departure from Christ	Repent, be an overcomer	Salvation–receive eternal life, Tree of Life
Smyrna (persecuted church 170–312)	Steadfast, poverty, persecution	Fear	Repent, be faithful, be an overcomer	Crown of life
Pergamos (wicked church 312–606)	Dwell in Satan's environment	Worship idols	Repent, be separate, be an overcomer	Hidden manna, new name
Thyatira (lax church 606–1520)	Some teach false doctrine, love	Sexual immortality	Repent, keep My works, be an overcomer	Power over the nations
Sardis (dead church 1520–1750)	Spiritually dead	Disobedient	Repent, hold fast, be an overcomer	Name written in the Book of Life
Philadelphia (favored church 1750–1900)	Holy believers	You have not denied Me	Repent, keep My works, be an overcomer	Write new name in New Jerusalem
Laodicea (lukewarm church 1900–Rapture)	Neither hot nor cold	Lukewarm	Repent, be zealous, be an overcomer	Sit on the throne with Jesus

1. The Church of Ephesus (Rev 2:1–7)

> [1]*"To the angel of the church of Ephesus write, 'These things says He who holds the seven stars in His right hand, who walks in the midst of the seven golden lampstands:* [2]*"I know your works, your labor, your patience, and that you cannot bear those who are evil. And you have tested those who say they are apostles and are not, and have found them liars;* [3]*and you have persevered and have patience, and have labored for My name's sake and have not become weary.* [4]*Nevertheless I have this against you, that you have left your first love.*

Condition and sin: Ephesus represents a backslidden church seen during the time of the apostles and the leaders that followed them. This period began in AD 70 when Jerusalem and the temple were burned and Jews sought refuge among the Gentile nations until approximately AD 170. John the apostle was the leader of the church of Ephesus. Ephesus is an example of a church that had divine knowledge and persevered for Christ, yet its members departed from the truth of the Word of God. They lost their first love, their goal to serve Christ.

- Gal 6:9: "And let us not grow weary while doing good, for in due season we shall reap if we do not lose heart."

> [5]*Remember therefore from where you have fallen; repent and do the first works, or else I will come to you quickly and remove your lampstand from its place—unless you repent.*

Work: They fell from grace and their dependence on Christ. The only way to Christ is through repentance. Repentance is seeing everything the way Jesus does, not with worldly thoughts, but spiritual. The Holy Spirit convicts us moment-by-moment.

> [6]*But this you have, that you hate the deeds of the Nicolaitans, which I also hate.* [7]*"He who has an ear, let him hear what the Spirit says to the churches. To him who overcomes I will give*

> *to eat from the tree of life, which is in the midst of the Paradise of God."'*

Reward: The Nicolaitans were an immoral group of Jerusalem church fathers according to Acts 6:5. The Lord cannot abide worldly thinking. The only way to heaven is to become an overcomer, the thing all the churches have in common, and the only way to do that is to be obedient to the leading of Christ. The word *overcomer* is mentioned eleven times in Revelation. We have the power and authority of the name of Jesus to overcome Satan, sin, sickness, and spiritual death. We can do all things through Christ who strengthens us (Phil 4:13). We must never give in to the power of Satan but rejoice continually as we see how Christ is blessing us in every circumstance. Satan cannot get to us if Jesus is between us. We know Jesus already defeated Satan, and as Ephesians chapter 1 says, Satan is under our feet. We are seated in heavenly places, on earth as it is in heaven. When Satan raises his head, we have but to say, "I rebuke you Satan in the name of Jesus; you have no way with me. Jesus is my Lord and Savior. Jesus, protect me and let me see how you are bringing me blessings through every experience. Praise You Jesus. Amen."

2. The Church of Smyrna (Rev 2:8–11)

> [8]*And to the angel of the church in Smyrna write, "These things says the First and the Last, who was dead, and came to life:* [9]*"I know your works, tribulation, and poverty (but you are rich); and I know the blasphemy of those who say they are Jews and are not, but are a synagogue of Satan.* [10]*Do not fear any of those things which you are about to suffer. Indeed, the devil is about to throw some of you into prison, that you may be tested, and you will have tribulation ten days. Be faithful until death, and I will give you the crown of life.*

Condition and sin: Smyrna represents the persecuted church seen during AD 170 to AD 312, a time of martyrdom. John speaks of those who were dead and came to life, the believers. They were in poverty, yet they had the wealth of spirituality. God sees those that rejected Christ as belonging to the worship of Satan. It says they will have tribulation ten days. The number ten stands for the law throughout the Bible and the length of Satan's testing.

The crown of life is one of the five crowns given in the New Testament in addition to the crown incorruptible, crown of righteousness, crown of rejoicing, and crown of glory. All the crowns are basically the same—when believers are resurrected to the bema seat judgment before Christ, they are crowned for the works the Holy Spirit accomplished through them while on earth. This happens when we look to the Holy Spirit for answers and then are obedient to follow His leading. We will never receive rewards for our good works. Only the works of the Holy Spirit are recognized in heaven.

- Jas 1:13: "Let no one say when he is tempted, 'I am tempted by God'; for God cannot be tempted by evil, nor does He Himself tempt anyone."

> [11a]*He who has an ear, let him hear what the Spirit says to the churches.*

Work: Hold fast, fear not, be faithful, and overcome all temptation.

- Mt 11:15: "He who has ears to hear, let him hear!"
- Rev 20:6: "Blessed and holy is he who has part in the first resurrection. Over such the second death has no power, but they shall be priests of God and of Christ, and shall reign with Him a thousand years."

> [11b] *He who overcomes shall not be hurt by the second death.*

Reward: These are the believers that will not face the great white throne judgment at the end of time. Again, those entering heaven have overcome Satan and haven't rejected Christ but are learning obedience to His Word.

3. The Church of Pergamos (Rev 2:12–17)

> [12]*And to the angel of the church in Pergamos write, "These things says He who has the sharp two-edged sword:"*

Condition and sin: Pergamos represents the licentious or wicked church seen during the time when the church created a religious system based on the Ten Commandments instead of a church that depended on Christ and the Holy Spirit, which still exists. Christ our Lord is the Word of God, the sword of the Lord. When we repeat the Word of God, it becomes a two-edged sword.

- Is 49:2: "And He had made My mouth like a sharp sword; in the shadow of His hand He has hidden Me, and made Me a polished shaft; in His quiver He has hidden Me."

> [13]*I know your works, and where you dwell, where Satan's throne is. And you hold fast to My name, and did not deny My faith even in the days in which Antipas was My faithful martyr, who was killed among you, where Satan dwells.* [14]*But I have a few things against you, because you have there those who hold the doctrine of Balaam, who taught Balak to put a stumbling block before the children of Israel, to eat things sacrificed to idols, and to commit sexual immorality.* [15]*Thus you also have those who hold the doctrine of the Nicolaitans, which thing I hate.* [16]*Repent, or else I will come to you quickly and will fight against them with the sword of My mouth.*

Work: Pergamos lived according to the world and not the Spirit. Persecution here is coming from within the church, the place where Satan has his throne. The idols had changed from Christ to worldly thoughts and possessions. In Ephesus, it referred to the Nicolaitans' deeds, but here, it has become doctrine. It has become religion, humanity's interpretation in each church. Christ will always be willing to hear our cry for repentance—this is seen throughout Revelation. Each church must stand on the gospel that Christ died, was buried, rose again, and is seated at the right hand of His Father in heaven. But more than that, a Christian is to follow Christ in obedience and depend upon the Holy Spirit, seeing everything as Jesus sees it—spiritually and not worldly.

- 1Co 6:13: "Foods for the stomach and the stomach for foods, but God will destroy both it and them. Now the body is not for sexual immortality but for the Lord, and the Lord for the body."
- 2Th 2:8: "And then the lawless one will be revealed, whom the Lord will consume with the breath of His mouth and destroy with the brightness of His coming."

> [17]*He who has an ear, let him hear what the Spirit says to the churches. To him who overcomes I will give some of the hidden manna to eat. And I will give him a white stone, and on the stone a new name written which no one knows except him who receives it.*

Reward: Those who can live in the world but not be of the world will be protected by Christ. There will be a new name for believers when they get to heaven.

- Ex 16:33–34: "And Moses said to Aaron, 'Take a pot and put an omer of manna in it, and lay it up before the Lord, to be kept for your generations. As the Lord commanded Moses, so Aaron laid it up before the Testimony, to be kept.'"

4. The Church of Thyatira (Rev 2:18–26)

> [18]*And to the angel of the church in Thyatira write, "These things says the Son of God, who has eyes like a flame of fire, and His feet like fine brass:* [19]*I know your works, love, service, faith, and your patience; and as for your works, the last are more than the first.* [20]*Nevertheless I have a few things against you, because you allow that woman Jezebel, who calls herself a*

prophetess, to teach and seduce My servants to commit sexual immorality and eat things sacrificed to idols."

Condition and sin: Thyatira represents a church seen from AD 606 to 1520 that was lax or tolerant. As the church goes into idolatry, it will suffer the consequences. We must be careful in choosing our church and make sure it is teaching the truth of the Word of God.

- Ex 34:13–16: "But you shall destroy their altars, break their sacred pillars, and cut down their wooden images (for you shall worship no other god, for the Lord, whose name is Jealous, is a Jealous God), lest you make a covenant with the inhabitants of the land, and they play the harlot with their gods and make sacrifice to their gods, and one of them invites you and you eat of his sacrifice, and you take of his daughters for your sons, and his daughters play the harlot with their gods and make your sons play the harlot with their gods."

21 And I gave her time to repent of her sexual immorality, and she did not repent. 22 Indeed I will cast her into a sickbed, and those who commit adultery with her into great tribulation, unless they repent of their deeds. 23 I will kill her children with death, and all the churches shall know that I am He who searches the minds and hearts. And I will give to each one of you according to your works.

Work: Sexual immorality is idolatry. Believers are to repent and see that Satan is behind all immorality. Still today, many in the church are not repentant as their own worldly needs come before a surrender to Jesus Christ to do all things as stated in the Word of God. Spending time with the Lord daily can lead only to repentance as the Holy Spirit reveals God's truth one day at a time.

The church still believes we can be good and go to heaven. That is a grave mistake. The Bible says only God is good. Our goodness comes only through the Holy Spirit, because in ourselves we can be only worldly.

The statement about being cast into a sickbed indicates that Satan overcomes those who do not know Christ by evil and demonic spirits. This mentality binds people with fear, anxiety, confusion, and legalism to the point of sickness. Over and over, we are told to repent and see things as Jesus does.

Romans chapter 1 shows the difference between the righteous and unrighteous. It says beginning in verse 28 that those who are unrighteous did not retain God in their knowledge, so God gave them over to debased minds to do unfitting things. Though they know the righteous judgment of God, those who practice such things are deserving of death; they not only do the same but also approve of those who practice them. Here in verse 23, God does not kill anyone with death but allows anyone who chooses to be unrighteous to fall to the clutches of Satan. In Romans chapter 1, God makes it clear that the unrighteous know the truth but choose worldliness instead of spiritual living.

- Jer 17:10: "I, the Lord, search the heart, I test the mind, even to give every man according to his ways, according to the fruit of his doings."

> *24Now to you I say, and to the rest in Thyatira, as many as do not have this doctrine, who have not known the depths of Satan, as they say, I will put on you no other burden. 25But hold fast what you have till I come. 26And he who overcomes, and keeps My works until the end, to him I will give power over the nations—He shall rule them with a rod of iron; as the potter's vessels shall be broken to pieces'—I also have received from My Father; and I will give him the morning star. He who has an ear, let him hear what the Spirit says to the churches.*

Reward: Do you know the depths of Satan? Satan is real, and we must know how he causes us to be less than obedient to Christ. The whole Old Testament was to let us know that God requires obedience. Obedience is to know Christ and His Word so we can honor it. If we don't know the truth of the Lord, then Satan has us by default because we are born in sin and under Satan's lordship since the sin of Adam.

Obedience is required today just as it was with Adam. The New

Testament teaches grace. Grace is not that we are saved and can do anything we want; grace is that Christ resides in us and that the Holy Spirit will convict us of the same character as Jesus Christ. It isn't that we won't sin; it is that we won't want to sin. We are made in the image of Christ. The Holy Spirit is our guide. Our challenge is to line up our soul (mind, will, and emotions) with the Holy Spirit within us.

Christ will keep His promises and will surely return so the church, His kings and priests, will rule and reign with Him throughout the millennium. Believers will become the bride of Christ and return to earth with Jesus, the Bridegroom. The Morning Star (Christ) burns brightly and gloriously.

The Jews were a part of the church as all the apostles were Jews. When we speak of the church, it is not to exclude the Jews who want to believe the Messiah has come. They are called Messianic Jews and do not become a part of the Gentile church; they are known as Christ believers who will go in the rapture—they are part of the church just as the disciples were. A Jew is considered one who believes the Messiah has not come.

- Ac 15:28–29: "For it seemed good to the Holy Spirit, and to us, to lay upon you no greater burden than these necessary things: that you abstain from things offered to idols, from blood, from things strangled, and from sexual immorality. If you keep yourselves from these, you will do well."
- Isa 32:1: "Behold, a king shall reign in righteousness, and princes shall rule in judgment."

5. The Church of Sardis (Rev 3:1–6)

> [1]*And to the angel of the church in Sardis write, "These things says He who has the seven Spirits of God and the seven stars: I know your works, that you have a name that you are alive, but you are dead."*

Condition and sin: Sardis represents a dead church that was seen as bringing forth the reformation in the 1500s. The seven spirits of God is the Holy Spirit in all the power and authority of the name of Jesus Christ.

The seven stars are pastors or leaders who are teaching from their hearts and not that of Jesus Christ.

- Jude 22–23: "And on some have compassion, making a distinction; but others save with fear, pulling them out of the fire, hating even the garment defiled by the flesh."

2Be watchful, and strengthen the things which remain, that are ready to die, for I have not found your works perfect before God. 3Remember therefore how you have received and heard; hold fast and repent. Therefore if you will not watch, I will come upon you as a thief, and you will not know what hour I will come upon you.

Work: We must have the baptism of the Holy Spirit in order to receive the anointing—the power and authority of the name of Jesus. We are to walk in the Spirit and not in the flesh. Remember, these words are to believers. We can have salvation without power, which means that when we face circumstances, we don't know to use the name of Jesus to protect us from Satan, sin, and sickness.

- 1Ti 6:20–21: "O Timothy! Guard what was committed to your trust, avoiding the profane and idle babblings and contradictions of what is falsely called knowledge— by professing it some have strayed concerning the faith."

4You have a few names even in Sardis who have not defiled their garments; and they shall walk with Me in white, for they are worthy. 5He who overcomes shall be clothed in white garments, and I will not blot out his name from the Book of Life; but I will confess his name before My Father and before His angels. 6'He who has an ear, let him hear what the Spirit says to the churches.'

Reward: Only when we walk in the Spirit can we overcome our flesh and receive the blessings of the cross.

6. *The Church of Philadelphia (Rev 3:7–13)*

> *[7]And to the angel of the church in Philadelphia write, "These things says He who is holy, He who is true, He who has the key of David, He who opens and no one shuts, and shuts and no one opens."*

Condition and sin: Philadelphia represents a favored church that began a missionary movement from 1750 and continues today. Philadelphia means brotherly love. These are those that walk in the Spirit and not in the flesh. The fruit of the Spirit (Gal 5:22) are the characteristics of Christ. They stand on the truth of the Word of God and are not ashamed of the gospel of Jesus Christ.

- Mt 16:19: "And I will give you the keys of the kingdom of heaven, and whatever you bind on earth will be bound in heaven, and whatever you loose on earth will be loosed in heaven."

> *[8]I know your works. See, I have set before you an open door, and no one can shut it; for you have a little strength, have kept My word, and have not denied My name. [9]Indeed I will make those of the synagogue of Satan, who say they are Jews and are not, but lie—indeed I will make them come and worship before your feet, and to know that I have loved you. [10]Because you have kept My command to persevere, I also will keep you from the hour of trial which shall come upon the whole world, to test those who dwell on the earth. [11]Behold, I am coming quickly! Hold fast what you have, that no one may take your crown.*

Work: Jesus commends those who have not denied Him. Here is the definition of being holy—one who keeps His commandments. Philadelphia is a holy, obedient church. Verse 9 addresses the Jews still under the lordship of Satan. However, Christ will bring the Jews to worship Him and give them grace when He restores Israel at the second coming. Christ will rapture those in the church who have persevered and have been obedient to His Word before the tribulation. When that happens, Satan will try to snatch up everyone left on earth. After all, every righteous person will be in heaven and only the unrighteous will remain on earth. Can you imagine the level of evil?

- 1Co 16:13–14: "Watch, stand fast in the faith, be brave, be strong. Let all that you do be done with love."

> [12]*He who overcomes, I will make him a pillar in the temple of My God, and he shall go out no more. I will write on him the name of My God and the name of the city of My God, the New Jerusalem, which comes down out of heaven from My God. And I will write on him My new name.* [13]*He who has an ear, let him hear what the Spirit says to the churches.*

Reward: The overcomer will not have to deal with this worldly evil any more. He shall go no more out from the presence and protection of God. Those with ears, let them hear. Do we hear that we must be spiritually ready for the rapture, which can come only by living through faith—trusting in God?

- 2Co 1:20–24: "For all the promises of God in Him are Yes, and in Him Amen, to the glory of God through us. Now He who establishes us with you in Christ and has anointed us is God, who also has sealed us and given us the Spirit in our hearts as a guarantee. Moreover I call God as witness against my soul, that to spare you I came no more to Corinth. Not that we have dominion over your faith, but are fellow workers for your joy; for by faith you stand."

7. The Church of Laodicea (Rev 3:14–22)

> [14]*And to the angel of the church of the Laodiceans write, "These things says the Amen, the Faithful and True Witness, the Beginning of the creation of God:* [15]*I know your works, that you are neither cold nor hot. I could wish you were cold or hot."*

Condition and sin: Laodicea represents a lukewarm church or the apostate church, which began in the 1900s and will last until the coming of Christ with the rapture. Being neither cold or hot means that as we see the demise of righteousness, we do nothing.

- Lk 12:35–37: "Let your waist be girded and your lamps burning; and you yourselves be like men who wait for their master, when he will return from the wedding, that when he comes and knocks they may open to him immediately. Blessed are those servants whom the master, when he comes, will find watching. Assuredly, I say to you that he will gird himself and have them sit down to eat, and will come and serve them."

> [16]*So then, because you are lukewarm, and neither cold nor hot, I will vomit you out of My mouth.* [17]*Because you say, 'I am rich, have become wealthy, and have need of nothing'—and do not know that you are wretched, miserable, poor, blind, and naked—* [18]*I counsel you to buy from Me gold refined in the fire, that you may be rich; and white garments, that you may be clothed, that the shame of your nakedness may not be revealed; and anoint your eyes with eye salve, that you may see.* [19]*As many as I love, I rebuke and chasten. Therefore be zealous and repent.*

Work: Are we praying for Christ to reign victoriously over our country and over the world? Those who are not walking in the Spirit but in the flesh will be discounted when Christ returns. Having no need for Christ is not being dependent upon the Lord, the teaching of the Bible. We cannot make a decision without Him. We look at our worldly success and wealth, and it characterizes us. Christ has already paid the price for every believer. We must be refined by God to take on His character (fruit of the Spirit in Galatians 5:22) and be clothed in righteousness. Even the church today is spiritually blind. God continues to offer repentance throughout Revelation. It is never too late to turn to Christ and away from our worldly ways that worship Satan and not God.

- Jn 14:23: "Jesus answered and said to him, 'If anyone loves Me, he will keep My word; and My Father will love him, and We will come to him and make Our home with him.'"
- 2Co 5:2-3: "For in this we groan, earnestly desiring to be clothed with our habitation which is from heaven, if indeed, having been clothed, we shall not be found naked."
- Col 1:15: "He is the image of the invisible God, the firstborn over all creation."

> *20Behold, I stand at the door and knock. If anyone hears My voice and opens the door, I will come in to him and dine with him, and he with Me. 21To him who overcomes I will grant to sit with Me on My throne, as I also overcame and sat down with My Father on His throne. 22He who has an ear, let him hear what the Spirit says to the churches.*

Reward: Christ paid the penalty for everyone, yet not everyone has claimed his or her freedom. Christ will not come and get them. The Bible says the truth is known. He is on the outside, but every person must open the door to Him. Many know how to give but not how to receive.

We cannot be proud; we must instead surrender to receive the gift of grace that Christ offers. But it is more than that. We must invite Him inside us and let Him know we want to be inside Him. This intimacy is the presence of Christ that overcomes the world. It isn't just salvation but allowing the Holy Spirit to lead us in His truth to receive the power and authority of the name of Jesus Christ. We need to plead the blood of Jesus into every circumstance and see that Jesus overcame Satan two thousand years ago. He is still victorious though all His saints; that we overcome the world today in His name.

How do we overcome? Satan, sin, sickness and spiritual death have no hold over us. We believe that the name of Jesus overcomes all and that we can reign victorious right now on earth as it is in heaven.

Why did Jesus leave us on earth after we were saved? Isaiah 43:7 says we were created for His glory. Every moment, we must have the mind of Christ and take every thought captive to overcome the world and walk spiritually, bringing victory to Christ and overcoming Satan and his evil. Praise You, Jesus!

The word *behold* can be taken as "Here I am!" John sees Jesus standing at the door. Jesus is beckoning all to believe and come to Him for eternal life. This beckoning is also to individuals in the church. Jesus has come to sup with us. He is offering an intimate relationship where He is the answer to everything—trust and obey, for there is no other way. Though Christ is on the throne, He is very much alive in all of our hearts as believers.

- Matthew 19:28–30: "So Jesus said to them, 'Assuredly I say to you, that in the regeneration, when the Son of Man sits on the Throne of His glory, you who have followed Me will also sit on twelve thrones, judging the twelve tribes of Israel. And everyone who has left houses or brothers or sisters or father or mother or wife or children or lands, for My name's sake, shall receive a hundredfold, and inherit eternal life. But many who are first will be last, and the last first.'"

CHAPTER 3

Revelation 4–5: Christ Receiving His Inheritance

The last three chapters are the hope of glory that those who have come to Christ God deems righteous (Ro 3:21–26); they exchanged their sin for the righteousness of God (2Co 5:21). Therefore, they are always ready to be caught up to heaven because they are the "redeemed." Chapter 4 is the rapture of the church, which completes the church age that takes us from the resurrection to the rapture, the time during which Christ has been preparing for His bride in His Father's house.

Now it is time to introduce all redeemed spirits individually to His Father and give them their glorified bodies and their new names in the kingdom of God. According to ancient Jewish wedding practices, they have already been considered one under the marriage contract. They have been a part of the kingdom of God since their salvation, but now they will witness firsthand, as John did, the majesty of their King.

Here is a snapshot of chapters four and five.

1. The Throne Room of Heaven (Rev 4:1)
2. First Judgment—Bema Seat Judgment (Rev 4:2–3)
3. Five Crowns (Rev 4:4–5a)
4. Seven Spirits of God (Rev 4:5b)
5. Four Living Creatures (Rev 4:6–11)
6. The Lamb Takes the Scroll (Rev 5:1–7)
7. Worthy is the Lamb (Rev 5:8–14)

1. The Throne Room of Heaven (Rev 4:1)

> [1]*After these things I looked* [introduction to an event], *and behold, a door standing open in heaven. And the first voice which I heard was like a trumpet speaking with me, saying, "Come up here, and I will show you things which must take place after this."*

"After this" means after the church age is ended. "After these things I looked" is used as an introduction to an event for John. Chapter 4 begins the "things which will take place." Now comes the time of celebration when the Bridegroom has brought His bride to His Father. He paid the price, the ransom for His church. All shall honor Jesus as the Christ (Phil 2:10). Christ is all the fullness of the Godhead seated at the right hand of the Father.

Christ is worthy and recognized by adoration to reign as King of Kings and Lord of Lords. A trumpet announced God to the people at Mount Sinai in Exodus 19:16, and we will hear the same trumpet sound each time the Lord has an angel announce a major event during the tribulation.

- Is 6:1: "In the year that King Uzziah died, I saw the Lord sitting on a throne, high and lifted up, and the train of His robe filled the temple."
- Jn 14:2–3: "In My Father's house are many mansions; if it were not so, I would have told you. I go to prepare a place for you. And if I go and prepare a place for you, I will come again and receive you to Myself; that where I am, there you may be also."
- Lk 17:34–36: "I tell you, in that night there will be two men in one bed: the one will be taken and the other will be left. Two women will be grinding together: the one will be taken and the other left. Two men will be in the field: the one will be taken and the other left."
- 1Co 15:22–26: "For as in Adam all die, even so in Christ all shall be made alive. But each one in his own order: Christ the firstfruits, afterward those who are Christ's at His coming. Then comes the

end, when He delivers the kingdom to God the Father, when He puts an end to all rule and all authority and power. For He must reign till He has put all enemies under His feet. The last enemy that will be destroyed is death."

- 1Co 15:51–52: "Behold, I tell you a mystery: We shall not all sleep, but we shall all be changed—in a moment, in the twinkling of an eye, at the last trumpet. For the trumpet will sound, and the dead will be raised incorruptible, and we shall be changed."
- 2Co 5:8: "We are confident, yes, well pleased rather to be absent from the body and to be present with the Lord."
- Eph 5:22–27: " Wives, submit to your own husbands, as to the Lord. For the husband is head of the wife, as also Christ is head of the church; and He is the Savior of the body. Therefore, just as the church is subject to Christ, so let the wives be to their own husbands in everything. Husbands, love your wives, just as Christ also loved the Church and gave Himself for her, that He might sanctify and cleanse her with the washing of water by the word, that He might present her to Himself a glorious Church, not having spot or wrinkle or any such thing, but that she should be holy and without blemish."
- Phil 3:20–21: "For our citizenship is in heaven, from which we also eagerly wait for the Savior, the Lord Jesus Christ, who will transform our lowly body that it may be conformed to His glorious body, according to the working by which He is able even to subdue all things to Himself."
- 1Th 4:16–17: "For the Lord Himself will descend from heaven with a shout, with the voice of an archangel, and with the trumpet of God. And the dead in Christ will rise first. Then we who are alive and remain shall be caught up together with them in the clouds to meet the Lord in the air. And thus we shall always be with the Lord."
- 1Th 2:7–8: "But we were gentle among you, just as a nursing mother cherishes her own children. So, affectionately longing for you, we were well pleased to impart to you not only the Gospel of God, but also our own lives, because you had become dear to us."

Trumpet is *salpinx* in Greek and is used to pronounce supernatural divine interpositions. Just like Jericho, every time we hear a trumpet sound in Revelation, it means judgment is coming against those who have lived their lives against the one true God. The voice John heard was none other than Jesus (Rev 1:10).

It doesn't say in Revelation that the rapture occurs. This is the mystery. It is for the Bible reader to read all Scripture and find where it is plugged in. This is the only place where the Scriptures above can relate. Verse 1 says the trumpet was sounded (1Th 4:16–17). Verse 4 says the twenty-four elders are sitting around the throne. They represent the priestly families of God (Old Testament and New Testament) in heaven. The fact that the elders are dressed in white means they are saints clothed in righteousness. Verse 5 says that the seven lamps, which has been described previously as the seven churches, has been removed from earth to heaven and are around the throne. This means the rapture had to have taken place at this time.

Just what happens in the rapture? In 1 Thessalonians 4:16 and 17, we read, "For the Lord Himself will descend from heaven with a shout … with the trumpet of God. The dead in Christ will rise first. [All the people who died before Christ but worshiped the One True God as their Lord, God deemed righteous. Paul made it clear all who were in paradise are released to heaven. Saints were seen released at the time of Christ's resurrection. Since Christ's resurrection, our loved ones have gone to heaven; 2 Corinthians 5:6–8 says that to be absent from the body is to be present with the Lord.] Then we who are alive and remain [those Christians alive] shall be caught up together with them in the clouds to meet the Lord in the air."

We will probably meet in the first heaven (clouds) and experience immediate human death (our spirit leaves our old body) and be transformed into our glorified body to enter heaven. All must die once (Heb 9:27), and 1 Corinthians 15:52–53 says that in the twinkling of an eye, at the last trump, we shall all be changed.

The restrainer is the prayers of the church through the Holy Spirit to restrain evil until the rapture, when the church is removed. The Holy Spirit will escort the church to heaven, but will He return to save multitudes throughout the tribulation? In 2 Thessalonians 2:7–8, we read,

"For the mystery of lawlessness is already at work; only He who now restrains will do so until He is taken out of the way. And then the lawless one will be revealed, whom the Lord will consume with the breath of His mouth and destroy with the brightness of His coming." Only the Holy Spirit can convict and bring saints to Jesus – many will be saved during the tribulation.

2. First Judgment—Bema Seat Judgment (Rev 4:2–3)

> [2]*Immediately I was in the Spirit; and behold, a throne set in heaven, and One sat on the throne.* [3]*And He who sat there was like a jasper and a sardius stone in appearance; and there was a rainbow around the throne, in appearance like an emerald.*

Jesus wants to give us a glimpse of how glorious it will be with Him for eternity. John saw a throne set in heaven (in the Holy of Holies—the seat of honor and glory, all power and authority), and One sat on the throne. Thou art worthy, O Lord, to receive glory and honor and power: for Thou has created all things, and for Thy pleasure they are and were created. He who sat there was like a jasper [not a human form but of transparent brightness] and a sardius stone in appearance [ruling in iron, this red stone signified justice] and there was a rainbow [Noah was given a rainbow to signify that the world would not be destroyed as in the past] around the throne in appearance like an emerald [green signifies the new covenant]. God is a covenant God who fulfills all of His promises in Revelation. Here we see God in all His glory.

The bema seat judgment will be where the word *works* for a Christian is understood. Our works in and of themselves never get us anything, especially not our salvation, as that is a gift from God through the shed blood of Jesus Christ. Our names were written in the Book of Life before the foundation of the world (Rev 17:8). The Holy Spirit convicted us that Christ is the one true God. The works of a Christian are those things we do through the conviction of the Holy Spirit. We are rewarded for every time we accept deliverance from Christ.

Salvation means deliverance, and just as in the Old Testament, every time an individual trusted, the Lord God blessed them. Now at the bema seat judgment, believers will receive their crowns based on their Christian works. We must ask ourselves how many people have we led to the Lord? How many seeds did we sow? How much did we love others and sacrifice ourselves that they would know Jesus? How many times did we shy away from giving the gospel message and take away someone's opportunity God had presented and we didn't do our Christian work?

Believers cannot be judged for sin because Jesus paid the price for our sin. How well did we give glory to God for giving us His righteousness and holiness and tell others of the goodness of God? Were we negative, complaining as did the Israelites in the wilderness because they didn't have leeks? Have we accepted our gift of deliverance today, every day, every minute? Or are we living in Satan's environment and not living in the victory of Jesus Christ? We saw over the last two chapters how Jesus will judge believers. Have we repented and asked Jesus to help us do our Christian work to be overcomers in the name of Jesus?

There is a rainbow surrounding the throne that is a sign of the Lord's covenant He made with Noah after the flood (Ge 8:20). In the New Testament, it is a sign of the covenant Christ made with His people. The colors of Noah's rainbow were red, orange, yellow, green, blue, indigo, and violet. The color around the throne is emerald. We live in the hope that we will see this rainbow that signifies Jesus will keep His covenant with us. God will fulfill His promises.

- Ez 1:28: "Like the appearance of a rainbow in a cloud on a rainy day, so was the appearance of the brightness all around it. This was the appearance of the likeness of the glory of the Lord. So when I saw it, I fell on my face, and I heard a voice of One speaking."
- Ro 14:10: "For we shall all stand before the judgment seat of Christ." The Greek noun *bema* is the judgment seat of God. At this *bema* believers are to be made manifest, that each may receive the things done in (or through) the body according to what he has done, whether it be good or bad. There they will receive rewards for their faithfulness to the Lord.
- 1Th 5:9–10: "For God did not appoint us to wrath, but to obtain salvation through our Lord Jesus Christ, who died for us, that whether we wake or sleep, we should live together with Him."

3. Five Crowns (Rev 4:4–5a)

> [4a]*Around the throne were twenty-four thrones, and on the thrones I saw twenty-four elders sitting, clothed in white robes;*

In 1 Chronicles 24:1–9, we read that twenty-four priests are dedicated to represent all the families of the priesthood. The elders represent the twelve tribes of Israel and the twelve apostles of Jesus. Revelation 21:10 describes New Jerusalem, where the twelve gates are named after the twelve tribes of Israel and the twelve foundation stones are named after the twelve apostles of Jesus.

> [4b]*and they had crowns of gold on their heads.*

At the bema seat judgment, believers will be rewarded with crowns based on their service to Christ in the world. It says we will throw our crowns at the foot of Jesus because all our rewards were based on His goodness and because we allowed Him to work through us to please His Father. Where will we be seated in the throne room? Obviously, the twenty-four elders are up front, and it could be that the closer we are to the Lord on earth, the closer we will be positioned to Him in the throne room. After this ceremony, the church will be praying during the tribulation, filling bowls of incense to be poured out (5:8). The bride of Christ will also be preparing for the return to earth after the seven-year tribulation, to rule and reign during the millennium with Christ as His priests and kings. I so look forward to being in heaven to hear about our next adventure in the realm of our journey with Christ.

- 2Co 5:9–10: "Therefore we will make it our aim, whether present or absent, to be well pleasing to Him. For we must all appear before the judgment seat of Christ, that each one may receive the things done in the body, according to what he has done, whether good or bad."

These are the five crowns or rewards spoken of in the New Testament:

- Crown incorruptible: And everyone who competes for the prize is temperate in all things. Now they do it to obtain a perishable crown, but we for an imperishable crown. (1Co 9:25–27)
- Crown of rejoicing: For what is our hope, or joy, or crown of rejoicing? Is it not even you in the presence of our Lord Jesus Christ at His coming? For you are our glory and joy. (1Th 2:19–20)
- Crown of righteousness: Finally, there is laid up for me the crown of righteousness, which the Lord, the righteous Judge, will give to me on that Day, and not to me only but also to all who have loved His appearing. (2Ti 4:8)
- Crown of life: Blessed is the man who endures temptation; for when he has been approved, he will receive the crown of life which the Lord has promised to those who love Him. (Jas 1:12)
- Crown of glory: and when the Chief Shepherd appears, you will receive the crown of glory that does not fade away. (1Pe 5:4)

The crowns of gold signify authority and represent the spiritual things Jesus Christ has asked us to do. Crowning is to give honor, recognition, and reward for one's achievements. Scripture makes us aware that we are rewarded, thanked, and appreciated for the love we share with others in His name. These works are acts of divine love believers pour on others. Realize that even though our family members have gone before us, all the church will be receiving their crowns together. This is the time of the bride of Christ when He is presenting His bride to His Father. The whole church was not together before; it is only now that the church age has ended. In 2 Timothy 4:8, we read that when the saints are gathered around the judgment seat of Christ, that is the day they will get their crowns.

Revelation 4:10 states that the elders cast their crowns before the throne. In ancient times, kings would lay their crowns before the emperors to show their allegiance. Jesus crowns us kings, and in return, like the elders, we cast our crowns before Christ. We are to experience that there is no crown like Jesus Christ. We are recognized first, and then we reciprocate. Is that not the way of God?

- 1Co 3:14: "If anyone's work which he has built on it endures, he will receive a reward."

> [5a]*And from the throne proceeded lightnings, thunderings, and voices: and there were seven lamps of fire burning before the throne, which are the seven spirits of God.*

In Exodus 19:16, when God gave the Law at Sinai, lightnings, thunderings and voices were present. Here are the thunderings again accompanied with lightnings. God is celebrating that the church (the seven lamps) is now around the throne. Luke 15:10 says, "There is joy in the presence of the angels of God over one sinner who repents." Each child born to God is a major event. Now His family is with Him.

4. Seven Spirits of God (Rev 4:5b)

> [5b]*Seven lamps of fire were burning before the throne, which are the seven Spirits of God.*

The number seven represents perfection and is the totality of the Holy Spirit. These lamps are the individuals as lamps in the seven lampstands in the church of God. The fire will purify them after this judgment with Christ. All the things that were not the work of Jesus will be consumed by fire. We will suffer loss and see missed opportunities in our lives. Jesus will take them all out of our conscience because there is no condemnation in Jesus Christ (Ro 8:1). Fire purifies. Suffering loss here could also mean that those who endured victoriously on earth will be positioned in God's kingdom accordingly.

- 1Co 3:9–15: "For we are God's fellow workers; you are God's field, you are God's building. According to the grace of God which was given to me, as a wise master builder I have laid the foundation, and another builds on it. But let each one take heed how he builds on it. For no other foundation can anyone lay than that which is laid, which is Jesus Christ. Now if anyone builds on this foundation with gold, silver, precious stones, wood, hay, straw, each one's *work* will become clear; for the Day will declare it, because it will be revealed by fire; and the fire will test each one's work, of what sort it is. If anyone's work which he has built on it endures, he will receive a reward. If anyone's work is burned, he will suffer loss; but he himself will be saved, yet so as through fire."

- Isa 11:1–2: "There shall come forth a rod out of the stem of Jesse, and a Branch shall grow out of his roots. The **SPIRIT OF THE LORD** shall rest upon him, the **SPIRIT OF WISDOM** and **UNDERSTANDING**, the **SPIRIT OF COUNSEL** and **MIGHT**, the **SPIRIT OF KNOWLEDGE** and of the **FEAR OF THE LORD**. (emphasis added)"

Did we have these seven spirits in us through the Holy Spirit when we were on earth? The same Spirit that raised Jesus from the dead dwells in us—the same Holy Spirit. This is how we will be judged as to whether we allowed the Holy Spirit to work through us. If this refers to our earthly walk, we know how we will be judged—only those things we did through the Holy Spirit will be worthy of reward. Certainly, we cannot bring our fleshly acts, so the acts we are rewarded for are those times when we surrender to Christ and are a vessel to do His work.

We pointed out in chapter 1 that these seven spirits describe the character of the Holy Spirit. They are the spirits that the Holy Spirit manifests in believers.

1. The Spirit of the Lord—the ability to have the same nature as Jesus
2. The Spirit of wisdom—the ability to walk in righteousness
3. The Spirit of understanding—the ability to have God's understanding in everything
4. The Spirit of counsel—the ability to surrender to the Holy Spirit's guidance
5. The Spirit of might—the ability to perform God's Word
6. The Spirit of knowledge—the ability to know how to walk in the Spirit and not in the flesh
7. The Spirit of the fear of the Lord—the ability to respect God's presence

5. Four Living Creatures (Rev 4:6–11)

> *6a Before the throne there was a sea of glass, like crystal.*

The sea of glass shows perfect transparency. The fact that they did not rest night or day shows they are spirit and not flesh.

Osborne[5] describes the sea of glass, "The most likely allusion here is the expanse or firmament that separated the waters in Genesis 1:7. Ezekiel 1:22 builds on Genesis 1:7 in describing an expanse, sparkling like ice, and awesome, above the living creatures. The Throne of God rested on this expanse. Crystal clear glass resembles a sea and adds to the imagery. John does not say that this sea exists in heaven but that what is there looks like a sea of glass. The emphasis is on God's awesome vastness, His transcendence and His holiness that separate Him from His creation (like the firmament separated the waters). The scene is enhanced greatly by this spectacular image. In one sense it is like glass, reflecting the magnificence and kaleidoscopic colors of the Throne Room. In another sense it is transparent, crystal clear, radiating his awesome holiness (not the crystal clear jasper of 21:11, the gold like pure glass of 21:18, and the crystal clear of the water of life of 22:1 in the description of the New Jerusalem). This sea appears two more times in the book at 15:2 the sea of glass is mingled with fire, pointing to divine judgment (as has every other image in this section); and in 21:1 we are told there was no longer any sea which may refer to the sea as the abyss, the chaos of the deep that in ancient times signified the reign of evil in this world. All three are interconnected with 4:5 the basis of the others. Here the crystal clear sea of glass symbolizes God's transcendent holiness and His awesome sovereignty that is a source of worship (4:6) and then becomes the basis of judgment (15:2) when God will eradicate evil from His creation (21:1)."

Isn't that awesome? The definition of *holiness* we know is to be separated from sin, separated unto God and not the world, walking in the Spirit and not in the flesh, spiritual thinking, not worldly. This ties into the sea of glass as a separation from sin. Here, as throughout the rest of the Bible, God is showing us His holiness.

> [6b]*And in the midst of the throne, and around the throne, were four living creatures full of eyes in front and in back.* [7]*The first living creature was like a lion, the second living creature like a calf, the third living creature had a face like a man, and the fourth living creature was like a flying eagle.* [8]*The four living creatures, each having six wings, were full of eyes around and within. And they do not rest day or night, saying: "Holy, holy, holy, Lord God Almighty, Who was and is and is to come!"*

- Isa 6:2–3: "Above it stood seraphim; each one had six wings: with two he covered his face, with two he covered his feet, and with two he flew. And one cried to another and said: 'Holy, holy, holy is the Lord of hosts; the whole earth is full of His glory!"
- Ez 1:10: "As for the likeness of their faces, each had the face of a man, each of the four had the face of a lion on the right side, each of the four had the face of an ox on the left side, and each of the four had the face of an eagle."
- Ez 10:14: "Each one had four faces: the first face was the face of a cherub, the second face the face of a man, the third the face of a lion, and the fourth the face of an eagle."

We see Christ portrayed in the four faces. By having all four, it depicts the fullness of Christ. These four living creatures protect the throne of God.

- The first living creature is like a lion. During the tribulation, Jesus will be like a lion, not a lamb.
- The second living creature is like a calf. The animal is used for sacrifice as Jesus was our sacrifice.
- The third living creature had a face like a man. Christ came to earth as a man in order that He might take on the sins of humanity.
- The fourth living creature was like a flying eagle. The eagle symbolizes the deity of Christ in God's sovereignty.

> [9]*Whenever the living creatures give glory and honor and thanks to Him who sits on the throne, who lives forever and ever,* [10]*the*

> *twenty-four elders fall down before Him who sits on the throne and worship Him who lives forever and ever, and cast their crowns before the throne, saying:* [11]*"You are worthy, O Lord, To receive glory and honor and power; For You created all things, And by Your will they exist and were created."*

We must get this picture. The throne is not against a wall as we vision King David; the throne is in the center of the Holy of Holies; it is the throne room of God (v. 2). The living creatures surround the throne, one on the left, right, front, and rear (v. 6). The twenty-four elders are in a circle around the living creatures at the throne (v. 4). The seven lamps are the Old Testament and New Testament saints who make up all of the redeemed (v. 5). They are all circled behind the twenty-four elders around the throne. Whenever the living creatures lead worship, the twenty-four elders fall down before Him and worship. The twenty-four elders are the leaders of the saints, so when they fall down and worship, the saints follow and all give homage to our Lord God, the King of Kings and Lord of Lords.

- 1Co 4:5: "Therefore judge nothing before the time, until the Lord comes, who will both bring to light the hidden things of darkness and reveal the counsels of the hearts. Then each one's praise will come from God." Our praise will come from God? He can do only good!
- Col 1:16: "For by Him all things were created that are in heaven and that are on earth, visible and invisible, whether thrones or dominions or principalities or powers. All things were created through Him and for Him."
- 1Pe 1:6–9: "In this you greatly rejoice, though now for a little while, if need be, you have been grieved by various trials, that the genuineness of your faith, being much more precious than gold that perishes, though it is tested by fire, may be found to praise, honor, and glory at the revelation of Jesus Christ, whom having not seen you love. Though now you do not see Him, yet believing, you rejoice with joy inexpressible and full of glory, receiving the end of your faith—the salvation of your souls."

The Greek *epainos* denotes that God will bestow praise to believers (1Co 4:5) after the judgment seat of Christ, according to each person's actions at the revelation of Jesus Christ (1Pe 1:7). Does God fill us with praise like He filled us with His love in our spiritual bodies on earth (Ro 5:5)? God surpasses our understanding. All this becomes our hope in glory. We will be able to praise Jesus with the praise of God as we can love humanity today with the love of Jesus. How exciting!

What a celebration! Everyone is rejoicing at the culmination of the seven lampstands (the church), which has been resurrected to the throne of God. The Old and New Testament saints, all those God deems righteous to this point, make up God's new kingdom people. The seven spirits of God symbolized the celebration of the fullness of the works of the kingdom. The four living creatures are standing guard leading the celebration for God that all humanity was to be redeemed in the church age have been safely carried to heaven. The twenty-four elders, the representatives of God's people, were casting their crowns before the throne in recognition that all was the work of God's Spirit. This would also be the time that we, the church, would be casting our crowns at the foot of Jesus as well in thanksgiving for the fullness of our entrance into the kingdom of God. All heaven is rejoicing; this is divine worship—to God be the glory, great things He has done.

6. The Lamb Takes the Scroll (Rev 5:1–7)

> [1]*And I saw in the right hand of Him who sat on the throne a scroll written inside and on the back, sealed with seven seals.*
> [2]*Then I saw a strong angel proclaiming with a loud voice, "Who is worthy to open the scroll and to loose its seals?"* [3]*And no one in heaven or on the earth or under the earth was able to open the scroll, or to look at it.* [4]*So I wept much, because no one was found worthy to open and read the scroll, or to look at it.* [5]*But one of the elders said to me, "Do not weep. Behold, the Lion of the tribe of Judah, the Root of David, has prevailed to open the scroll and to loose its seven seals."*

Revelation 5 continues the celebration around the throne. The church recognizes Jesus as its King. It is time to receive the title deed to His inheritance—the scroll sealed with seven seals. Christ will repossess the earth previously ruled by Satan, who was called the god of this age (2Co 4:4). This will be the wedding gift to Christ's bride.

The right hand signifies power. The opening of the seven seals signifies that the judgment upon the earth or time of trouble for the Israelites or the tribulation has begun. The strong angel in verse 2 is probably Gabriel as seen in the book of Daniel. We now see Jesus, the Lion of the tribe of Judah, the root of David, receiving His reward for His works—as the sacrificial Lamb to bring redemption to God's people.

God had to wait until the elders or human witnesses were before God's court; hence, after the rapture, in order to represent the redeemed of Christ, Christ had been seated for the last two thousand years. Now He stands to command His rule of the kingdom of God. He is ready to assume the role of His new kingship.

> *6And I looked, and behold [intro a new event], in the midst of the throne and of the four living creatures, and in the midst of the elders, stood a Lamb as though it had been slain, having seven horns and seven eyes, which are the seven Spirits of God sent out into all the earth. 7Then He came and took the scroll out of the right hand of Him who sat on the throne.*

Seven horns indicate the fullness of power—He is omnipotent. Seven eyes indicate the fullness of knowledge—He is all knowing. The Lamb represents Christ's first coming, but now He is the Lion standing to lead the battle for His inheritance. We know the victory was won two thousand years ago, and it is now that Christ can claim all of His people who devoted themselves to Him to make up the kingdom of God.

7. Worthy is the Lamb (Rev 5:8–14)

> *8Now when He had taken the scroll, the four living creatures and the twenty-four elders fell down before the Lamb, each having a harp, and golden bowls full of incense, which are the prayers of the saints. 9And they sang a new song, saying: "You are worthy to take the scroll, And to open its seals; For You were*

> *slain, And have redeemed us to God by Your blood out of every tribe and tongue and people and nation, [10]And have made us kings and priests to our God; And we shall reign on the earth."*

Only Jesus is worthy. Christ's sacrificial death becomes His victory. Those who were slain are the tribulation saints. Here is the harp used in the Old Testament to sing the psalms (Ps 33:2). The bowls of incense are the prayers of the saints who were raptured before the tribulation. These are answered prayers from the church during the tribulation. The new song is for something new—the celebration of Christ's victory of the tribulation even before it begins. The scroll will be revealed, one judgment at a time. He is judge of the earth (Jn 5:22).

- Ex 19:6: "And you shall be to Me a kingdom of priests and a holy nation. These are the words which you shall speak to the children of Israel."
- Is 53:7: "He was oppressed and He was afflicted, yet He opened not His mouth; He was led as a lamb to the slaughter, and as a sheep before its shearers is silent, so He opened not His mouth."
- Is 61:6: "But you shall be named the Priests of the Lord, men shall call you the servants of our God. You shall eat the riches of the Gentiles, and in their glory you shall boast."
- Jn 1:29: "The next day John saw Jesus coming toward him, and said, 'Behold! The lamb of God who takes away the sin of the world!'"
- Phil 2:9–11: "Therefore God also has highly exalted Him and given Him the name which is above every name, that at the name of Jesus every knee should bow, of those in heaven, and of those on earth, and of those under the earth, and that every tongue should confess that Jesus Christ is Lord, to the glory of God the Father."

> *[11]Then I looked, and I heard the voice of many angels around the throne, the living creatures, and the elders; and the number of them was ten thousand times ten thousand, and thousands of thousands, [12]saying with a loud voice: "Worthy is the Lamb*

who was slain to receive power and riches and wisdom, And strength and honor and glory and blessing!" [13]*And every creature which is in heaven and on the earth and under the earth and such as are in the sea, and all that are in them, I heard saying: "Blessing and honor and glory and power Be to Him who sits on the throne, And to the Lamb, forever and ever!"* [14]*Then the four living creatures said, "Amen!" And the twenty-four elders fell down and worshiped Him who lives forever and ever.*

Jesus has a sevenfold inheritance, so He receives sevenfold praise.

1. Power—authority as God
2. Wealth—everything is His
3. Wisdom—holds the universe together
4. Strength—Creator of all things
5. Honor—respect from all His people
6. Glory—He is the image of God
7. Praise—worthy of all worship

The number ten thousand times ten thousands and thousands of thousands means a myriad of people, innumerable for John.

We realize all heaven celebrates at each major event, but we see this as the most significant. In the Old Testament, we saw kings co-reign with their sons. They were not given the title of king until the prior king appointed that time to their son. We realize that the twenty-four elders represent all righteous humanity and that the four living creatures represents all the righteous celestial beings, or actually all the righteous spirits God created.

God's kingdom spirits are all celebrating together. It is now that Christ is ready to read the scroll. Christ has received His inheritance, and it is now time to judge those upon the earth who rejected the truth that Jesus Christ was and is and always will be the Lord, the Son of God, and the Almighty who created all things and will continue to maintain all things.

As Jesus opens the seals, the four living creatures will release the first four judgments. Remember Jesus is in control from heaven, and the four living creatures (His angelic beings) are releasing these judgments upon the earth.

CHAPTER 4

Revelation 6–7: The Seal Judgments

First Seal (6:1–2)	Antichrist will come on a **white horse** (as deceiver) to rule the earth after the rapture; this begins the seven-year tribulation.
Second Seal (6:3–4)	Antichrist will come on a **red horse** and bring persecution.
Third Seal (6:5–6)	Antichrist will come on a **black horse** and bring worldwide famine.
Fourth Seal (6:7–8)	Antichrist will come on a **pale horse** and will bring death to a quarter of the world's population.
Fifth Seal (6:9–11)	Antichrist will bring martyrdom to those who will not worship him.
Sixth Seal (6:12–17)	God brings cosmic disorder; earthquake; sun will turn black; moon will turn red; stars will fall from the sky; so great will be the terror that the people will cry out to end the wrath.
Seventh Seal (7:1–17)	God will seal His people.

Chapter 4 was the rapture of the church, and chapter 5 was the celebration of Jesus receiving His inheritance, which is the plan to roll out the tribulation with the twenty-one judgments: seven seal judgments, seven trumpet judgments, and seven bowl judgments. Therefore, this is the beginning of the tribulation. Revelation 3:10 tells us the Lord will keep us from the hour of trial. The church is in heaven. But there is a shift now to earth as Jesus' judgments are upon the people on earth. We move back and forth from heaven to earth chapter by chapter throughout Revelation. In heaven, Jesus reveals what will take place, all heaven celebrates, and then we move to earth to see it played out.

After the rapture, when it is seen that the church has been removed from the earth, those who did not recognize Jesus will be persecuted under the Antichrist on earth. God will allow the Hebrew nation to be punished for rejecting the Godhead until many will be converted and accept Christ as their Messiah. When it is understood that the rapture indeed did happen, it will be the greatest outpouring of believers from all nationalities who want to be saved. It will be too late to leave in the rapture but not too late to escape the lake of fire. This decision will still have to be made by each individual (Jer 30:7).

- Jer 30:4–7: "Now these are the words that the LORD spoke concerning Israel and Judah. For thus says the LORD: 'We have heard a voice of trembling, of fear, and not of peace. Ask now, and see, whether a man is ever in labor with child? So why do I see every man with his hands on his loins like a woman in labor, and all faces turned pale? Alas! For that day is great, so that none is like it; and it is the time of Jacob's trouble, but he shall be saved out of it.'"

Zechariah prophesied in 1:8–11 and 6:1–8 of the restoration of Israel. Zechariah saw four angels riding horses to bring forth God's wrath on the earth that experienced corruption. Four chariots are drawn by red, sorrel (black), white, and dapple (gray) horses. While the evil spirits are riding on these horses, the people on earth still believe that Antichrist came in peace.

- Zec 1:8–11: "I saw by night, and behold, a man riding on a red horse, and it stood among the myrtle trees in the hollow; and behind him were horses: red, sorrel, and white. Then I said, 'My lord, what are these?' So the angel who talked with me said to me, 'I will show you what they are.' And the man who stood among the myrtle trees answered and said, 'These are the ones whom the LORD has sent to walk to and fro throughout the earth.' So they answered the Angel of the LORD, who stood among the myrtle trees, and said, 'We have walked to and fro throughout the earth, and behold, all the earth is resting quietly.'"

Zechariah saw mountains of bronze. The brazen altar symbolized judgment. Therefore, the four horses are spirits or angels of heaven the Lord will use for judgment. When he speaks of north and south, everything is from the center of Israel.

- Zec 6:1–8: "Then I turned and raised my eyes and looked, and behold, four chariots were coming from between two mountains, and the mountains were mountains of bronze. With the first chariot were red horses, with the second chariot black horses, with the third chariot white horses, and with the fourth chariot dappled horses—strong steeds. Then I answered and said to the angel who talked with me, 'What are these, my lord?' [5] And the angel answered and said to me, 'These are four spirits of heaven, who go out from their station before the Lord of all the earth. The one with the black horses is going to the North Country, the white are going after them, and the dappled are going toward the south country.' Then the strong steeds went out, eager to go, that they might walk to and fro throughout the earth. And He said, 'Go, walk to and fro throughout the earth.' So they walked to and fro throughout the earth. And He called to me, and spoke to me, saying, 'See, those who go toward the North Country have given rest to My Spirit in the North Country.'"

Up until the time of the rapture, the church was the restrainer through the Holy Spirit. Jesus could not judge the world until His people were under His protection. The falling away of the church (2Th 2:3–7) was the sign that the end times had arrived. Jesus from His throne will direct the operations of the tribulation through His angels. The church is in heaven preparing to return for the second coming with Jesus after the seven-year tribulation. Chapter 6 begins with the vision of what will happen on earth during this time.

- 2Th 2:3–7: "Let no one deceive you by any means; for that Day will not come unless the falling away comes first, and the man of sin is revealed, the son of perdition, who opposes and exalts himself above all that is called God or that is worshiped, so that he sits as God in the temple of God, showing himself that he is God. Do you not remember that when I was still with you I told you these things? And now you know what is restraining, that he may be revealed in his own time. For the mystery of lawlessness is already at work; only He who now restrains will do so until He is taken out of the way."

The seals are opened and contain the seven seal judgments; the seventh seal opens up the seven trumpet judgments, and then the seventh trumpet judgment opens up the seven bowl judgments. Each seal is released one by one consecutively throughout chapters six to nineteen.

1 seal judgments
2
3
4
5
6
7----------1 trumpet judgments
    2
    3
    4
    5
    6
    7----------1 bowl (vial) judgments
        2
        3
        4
        5
        6
        7 Return of Christ for Armageddon

1. First Seal (Rev 6:1–2)

> *[1]Now I saw when the Lamb opened one of the seals; and I heard one of the four living creatures saying with a voice like thunder, "Come and see." [2]And I looked, and behold, a white horse. He who sat on it had a bow; and a crown was given to him, and he went out conquering and to conquer.*

The first seal reveals the Antichrist coming on a white horse (disguised in white) to rule on earth after the rapture. The bow is a symbol of military strength, but the bow without arrows does not show the fight in him. He begins by deceiving Israel into accepting a peace treaty for seven years (Da 9:27).

DeYoung[4] gives great insight on this treaty, "I always taught that the Antichrist would sign a peace treaty. But, that's not what the text says. Daniel 9:27 says he shall confirm the covenant. The word in Hebrew is *gabar.* Never is it translated signed, it's always translated confirm, strengthen or make stronger. So, what we are looking at is a peace treaty or three of them on the table, not working, but waiting for somebody to come along and confirm them; make them work." DeYoung defined these three peace treaties that have already been signed as 1) The Camp David Accords in 1979, 2) the Oslo Accords in 1993, and 3) the peace treaty in 1994 with Jordan.

The crown described here is the Greek *stephanos*, a victor's crown or wreath given to the winner of the Greek games. King Jesus will wear a diadem, a crown that says he is King of Kings after He defeats Satan on earth.

Notice that we the church will never see the Antichrist revealed in our age. It is only after the tribulation has begun, when the church is in heaven, that the Antichrist will be revealed. It is the Lamb that opened the seal. Jesus says it, and then it happens just as He created the world in Genesis 1. He is the Word of God.

- Da 9:27: "Then he shall confirm a covenant with many for one week; But in the middle of the week He shall bring an end to sacrifice and offering. And on the wing of abominations shall be one who makes desolate, even until the consummation, which is determined, is poured out on the desolate."

- Mt 24:5: "For many will come in My name, saying, 'I am the Christ,' and will deceive many."

2. Second Seal (Rev 6:3–4)

> *[3]When He opened the second seal, I heard the second living creature saying, "Come and see." [4]Another horse, fiery red, went out. And it was granted to the one who sat on it to take peace from the earth, and that people should kill one another; and there was given to him a great sword.*

The second seal will reveal the Antichrist on a red horse who will begin persecution. The sword is a symbol of war, and the red horse indicates bloodshed as the Antichrist goes forth conquering and to conquer (Da 7:24, 11:40–45; Mt 24:6–7). We must remember that everyone on the earth after the rapture does not know Christ. There will be much confusion. Those people in the churches who thought they were saved but were not will learn the truth, and the greatest harvest will happen when the hearts of the father will be turned to the children and the children to the fathers (Mal 4:6). The Antichrist will turn on Israel with the intent to persecute and annihilate all Israel.

3. Third Seal (Rev 6:5–6)

> *[5]When He opened the third seal, I heard the third living creature say, "Come and see." So I looked, and behold [Intro to a new event], a black horse, and he who sat on it had a pair of scales in his hand. [6]And I heard a voice in the midst of the four living creatures saying, "A quart of wheat for a denarius, and three quarts of barley for a denarius; and do not harm the oil and the wine."*

The third seal will reveal Antichrist on a black horse representing sorrow. War had broken out with the red horse (second seal), which caused worldwide famine. The scales will be used to mete out food. A denarius was a penny, a day's wage for a laborer in John's day. With economic disaster, there won't be enough money to survive.

- Lev 26:26: "When I have cut off your supply of bread, ten women shall bake your bread in one oven, and they shall bring back your bread by weight, and you shall eat and not be satisfied."
- Ez 4:16–17: "Moreover He said to me, 'Son of man, surely I will cut off the supply of bread in Jerusalem; they shall eat bread by weight and with anxiety, and shall drink water by measure and with dread, that they may lack bread and water, and be dismayed with one another, and waste away because of their iniquity.'"

4. Fourth Seal (Rev 6:7–8)

> *7 When He opened the fourth seal, I heard the voice of the fourth living creature saying, "Come and see." 8 So I looked, and behold [intro to new event], a pale horse. And the name of him who sat on it was Death, and Hades followed with him. And power was given to them over a fourth of the earth, to kill with sword, with hunger, with death, and by the beasts of the earth.*

The fourth seal will reveal the Antichrist on a pale horse (the color of death) that will cause a fourth of the world's population to die. The world population as of May 11, 2011, was 6,852,472,823; a quarter of that is 1,713,118,206. According to the U.S. Census Bureau, the world population will increase approximately 1 billion people every ten years, reaching over 9 billion people by the year 2050.

Aune[1] gives light on death and Hades, "The name of the cavalier was Death, and Hades was following after him. Death is personified four times in Revelation (1:18, 6–8, 20:13, 14). And each time it is linked to a personified Hades. Since Death always comes before Hades in those four references, it is probable that Death is considered the one who reigns over Hades; i.e., Death is a person while Hades is his kingdom."

5. Fifth Seal (Rev 6:9–11)

> [9]*When He opened the fifth seal, I saw under the altar the souls of those who had been slain for the word of God and for the testimony which they held.* [10]*And they cried with a loud voice, saying, "How long, O Lord, holy and true, until You judge and avenge our blood on those who dwell on the earth?"* [11]*Then a white robe was given to each of them; and it was said to them that they should rest a little while longer, until both the number of their fellow servants and their brethren, who would be killed as they were, was completed.*

The fifth seal will reveal Antichrist, who will martyr those who do not worship him. The four living creatures summoned the four housemen of the Apocalypse where the Antichrist caused war upon the people. In the fifth seal, Christ will deal with the people who have been slain and then bring cosmic destruction upon those under the Antichrist.

- Heb 11:40: "God having provided something better for us that they should not be made perfect apart from us."
- Mt 24:9: "Then they will deliver you up to tribulation and kill you, and you will be hated by all nations for My name's sake."

The souls of the believers are gathered under the altar. They were slain for the Word of God and their testimony. Christians will seek to know the truth and choose Jesus over Satan. God will open the eyes of the Jews, and they will choose Jesus over the Antichrist. Realize that their spirits and souls are very much alive and their physical bodies have died. They are waiting for their glorified bodies. Their cry is like that of Psalm 94:1–3: "O Lord God, to whom vengeance belongs – O God, to whom vengeance belongs, shine forth! Rise up, O Judge of the earth; render punishment to the proud. Lord, how long will the wicked, how long will the wicked triumph?" These martyrs will receive white robes signifying the righteousness of Jesus. These believers will all be raptured at the same time so all heaven can welcome them around the throne in rejoicing.

6. Sixth Seal (Rev 6:12–17)

> *[12]I looked when He opened the sixth seal, and behold, there was a great earthquake; and the sun became black as sackcloth of hair, and the moon became like blood. [13]And the stars of heaven fell to the earth, as a fig tree drops its late figs when it is shaken by a mighty wind. [14]Then the sky receded as a scroll when it is rolled up, and every mountain and island was moved out of its place. [15]And the kings of the earth, the great men, the rich men, the commanders, the mighty men, every slave and every free man, hid themselves in the caves and in the rocks of the mountains, [16]and said to the mountains and rocks, "Fall on us and hide us from the face of Him who sits on the throne and from the wrath of the Lamb! [17]For the great day of His wrath has come, and who is able to stand?"*

The sixth seal will reveal the heavenlies bringing about a cataclysmic disaster. The earth will quake, the sun will turn black, the moon will turn red, the stars will fall from the sky, and so great will be the terror that the people will cry out to end this wrath. It looks like the earth's axis may have changed and caused everything on earth to be shifted. Many commentaries speak of a nuclear war, but Scripture says it is an earthquake from heaven, so that is what I believe. The stars could be, as commentators say, a meteor shower that drops in quantity like ripened figs fall with a mighty wind. But do you hear who those on earth blame? God, of course. They do not look to themselves and repent but shake their fists at God. They know the great day of wrath has come, the tribulation. How can they know of the tribulation that is told of in the Bible and yet not repent?

- Ps 2:2–4: "The kings of the earth set themselves, and the rulers take counsel together, against the Lord and against His Anointed, saying, 'Let us break their bonds in pieces and cast away their cords from us.'"
- Is 2:10: "Enter into the rock, and hide in the dust, from the terror of the Lord and the glory of His majesty."

- Is 24:21: "It shall come to pass in that day that the Lord will punish on high the host of exalted ones, and on the earth the kings of the earth."
- Zep 1:14: "The great day of the Lord is near; it is near and hastens quickly. The noise of the day of the Lord is bitter; there the mighty men shall cry out."
- Lk 23:29–30: "For indeed the days are coming in which they will say, 'Blessed are the barren, wombs that never bore, and breasts which never nursed!'"

The seventh judgment always brings forth another set of judgments. The seventh seal judgment kicks off the first trumpet judgment.

7. Seventh Seal (Rev 7:1–17)

Israel is sealed

> *[1]After these things I saw four angels standing at the four corners of the earth, holding the four winds of the earth, that the wind should not blow on the earth, on the sea, or on any tree. [2]Then I saw another angel ascending from the east, having the seal of the living God. And he cried with a loud voice to the four angels to whom it was granted to harm the earth and the sea, [3]saying, "Do not harm the earth, the sea, or the trees till we have sealed the servants of our God on their foreheads."*

These could be the same angels that were the spirits of the four horsemen. The four winds led the horses in the directions Jesus wanted them to go. These angels will seal God's people from harm and give them protection and provision just as the Israelites were protected through their wilderness journey. Later, the Antichrist will seal his people to copy what God did (Rev 16–18). This sealing is not a new thing; believers were sealed with the Holy Spirit.

- Mt 24:31: "And He will send His angels with a great sound of a trumpet, and they will gather together His elect from the four winds, from one end of heaven to the other."

- Jn 6:27: "Do not labor for the food which perishes, but for the food which endures to everlasting life, which the Son of Man will give you, because God the Father has set His seal on Him."
- 2Co 1:21-22: "Now He who establishes us with you in Christ and has anointed us is God, who also has sealed us and given us the Spirit in our hearts as a guarantee."
- Eph 1:13-14: "In Him you also trusted, after you heard the word of truth, the Gospel of your salvation; in whom also, having believed, you were sealed with the Holy Spirit of promise, who is the guarantee of our inheritance until the redemption of the purchased possession, to the praise of His glory."
- Eph 4:30: "And do not grieve the Holy Spirit of God, by whom you were sealed for the day of redemption."

> 4 *And I heard the number of those who were sealed. One hundred and forty-four thousand of all the tribes of the children of Israel were sealed:*
> 5 *of the tribe of Judah twelve thousand were sealed;*
> *of the tribe of Reuben twelve thousand were sealed;*
> *of the tribe of Gad twelve thousand were sealed;*
> 6 *of the tribe of Asher twelve thousand were sealed;*
> *of the tribe of Naphtali twelve thousand were sealed;*
> *of the tribe of Manasseh twelve thousand were sealed;*
> 7 *of the tribe of Simeon twelve thousand were sealed;*
> *of the tribe of Levi twelve thousand were sealed;*
> *of the tribe of Issachar twelve thousand were sealed;*
> 8 *of the tribe of Zebulun twelve thousand were sealed;*
> *of the tribe of Joseph twelve thousand were sealed;*
> *of the tribe of Benjamin twelve thousand were sealed.*

The first half of the tribulation is to be judgment on the Jews for three and a half years. During this time, God protects a remnant of Jews to carry the gospel message and to save multitudes of Jews and Gentiles during the tribulation. These 144,000 will be raptured before the bowl judgments are disbursed (Rev 14) when God destroys the world we know and regenerates it in preparation for the millennium. God will always protect His people and keep a remnant of the tribes; 12,000 people in twelve tribes equals 144,000 and symbolizes the complete fulfillment for Israel. It does not necessarily mean 144,000 people but symbolizes all Israel—the nation of Israel is being protected. The reason for the tribulation is for Israel to repent and turn to God.

A Multitude from the Great Tribulation Are Raptured

> *[9]After these things I looked, and behold [Intro of a new event], a great multitude which no one could number, of all nations, tribes, peoples, and tongues, standing before the throne and before the Lamb, clothed with white robes, with palm branches in their hands, [10]and crying out with a loud voice, saying, "Salvation belongs to our God who sits on the throne, and to the Lamb!" [11]All the angels stood around the throne and the elders and the four living creatures, and fell on their faces before the throne and worshiped God, [12]saying: "Amen! Blessing and glory and wisdom, Thanksgiving and honor and power and might, Be to our God forever and ever. Amen." [13]Then one of the elders answered, saying to me, "Who are these arrayed in white robes, and where did they come from?" [14]And I said to him, "Sir, you know." So he said to me, "These are the ones who come out of the great tribulation, and washed their robes and made them white in the blood of the Lamb. [15]Therefore they are before the throne of God, and serve Him day and night in His temple. And He who sits on the throne will dwell among them. [16]They shall neither hunger anymore nor thirst anymore; the sun shall not strike them, nor any heat; [17]for the Lamb who is in the midst of the throne will shepherd them and lead them to living fountains of waters. And God will wipe away every tear from their eyes."*

These are the martyrs that John saw under the altar in 6:9. These are the souls who had been slain for the Word of God and for the testimony; they will be raptured to the throne of God all at one time. They had white robes and were told there was a specific time for them. They are standing before the throne and are so thankful that they did not have to go to hell that they serve the Lord day and night in His temple.

- Ps 3:8: "Salvation belongs to the Lord. Your blessing is upon Your people."
- Ps 121:6: "The sun shall not strike out by day, nor the moon by night."
- Isa 4:4–6: "When the Lord has washed away the filth of the daughters of Zion, and purged the blood of Jerusalem from her midst, by the spirit of judgment and by the spirit of burning, then the Lord will create above every dwelling place of Mount Zion, and above her assemblies, a cloud and smoke by day and the shining of a flaming fire by night. For over all the glory there will be a covering. And there will be a Tabernacle for shade in the daytime from the heat, for a place of refuge, and for a shelter from storm and rain."
- Isa 49:10: "They shall neither hunger nor thirst, neither heat nor sun shall strike them; for He who has mercy on them will lead them, even by the springs of water He will guide them."
- Heb 9:13–14: "For if the blood of bulls and goats and the ashes of a heifer, sprinkling the unclean, sanctifies for the purifying of the flesh, how much more shall the blood of Christ, who through the eternal Spirit offered Himself without spot to God, cleanse your conscience from dead works to serve the living God?"

Now that Israel is sealed and the martyrs have been raptured, the Antichrist will be furious and stop anyone not dedicated to him from receiving food. Anyone not under the Antichrist will be martyred.

It is important to recognize that there are different dispensations and therefore different groups around the throne at this time. There were the Old Testament saints, New Testament saints, then the church, and now we have the tribulation saints. More Jews and Gentiles are yet to be resurrected as we move through God's plan.

CHAPTER 5

Revelation 8–11: The Trumpet Judgments

First Trumpet (8:7)	One-third of the earth's vegetation will be destroyed with hail and fire with blood, one-third of the sea creatures will die, and one-third of the ships will be destroyed.
Second Trumpet (8:8)	One-third of the seas will turn to blood.
Third Trumpet (8:10)	One-third of the fresh water rivers will become contaminated.
Fourth Trumpet (8:12)	One-third of the sun, moon, and stars will be darkened and the day will not shine for a third part of the day.
Fifth trumpet (9:1) First Woe	Demon locusts will inflict those with the mark of the Beast for five months.
Sixth Trumpet (9:13) Second Woe	One-third of humanity will be slayed by an army of two hundred million, yet they will not repent.
Seventh Trumpet (11:15) Third Woe	Seven thunders will occur, and the glory of the kingdom of Christ will be announced.

The previous seven seal judgments were broken down into two distinct parts: the four horsemen followed by three woes of cosmic changes. We will see the same pattern here of four judgments followed by three woes. A woe is a deep sorrow, grief, or affliction. The seventh seal kicks off the first new set of judgments.

The Antichrist stands up in the temple and demands worship at the midpoint of the tribulation. The first wave of tribulation saints have been raptured, and the 144,000 Jews have been protected. Each set of judgments worsens.

Seventh Seal (Rev 8:1–6)

> *[1]When He opened the seventh seal, there was silence in heaven for about half an hour. [2]And I saw the seven angels who stand before God and to them were given seven trumpets. [3]Then another angel, having a golden censer, came and stood at the altar. He was given much incense that he should offer it with the prayers of all the saints upon the golden altar which was before the throne. [4]And the smoke of the incense, with the prayers of the saints, ascended before God from the angel's hand. [5]Then the angel took the censer, filled it with fire from the altar, and threw it to the earth. And there were noises, thunderings, lightnings, and an earthquake. [6]So the seven angels who had the seven trumpets prepared themselves to sound.*

The half an hour of silence causes a break; God's wrath is ready to be poured out on all those who rejected His Son. Chapters 5–7 were the plan; now, we will see it implemented. God will allow the Antichrist to persecute those who turned away from God and were given every chance to repent but chose not to.

- 2Sa 22:8: "Then the earth shook and trembled; the foundations of heaven quaked and wee shaken, because He was angry."
- 2Ch 29:25–28: "And He stationed the Levites in the house of the Lord with cymbals, with stringed instruments, and with harps, according to the commandment of David, of Gad the king's seer, and of Nathan the prophet; for thus was the commandment of the Lord by His prophets."

Many commentaries state that this could be a nuclear attack by Satan, but we must not take what is written out of context. This is God's judgment; He is organizing this event. It is His angel who is throwing fire from the sky just as the Lord rained fire and brimstone on Sodom and Gomorrah out of the heavens (Ge 19:34).

The seven angels are ready to sound the trumpet to begin each judgment. Prayers are coming in agreement with God's will, and the saints have prayed for this very moment when Jesus would reign victoriously. Jesus is fighting for His inheritance as He wants to present it to His bride as a wedding present. God is about to destroy everything on earth so He can start again. God will destroy the corruption Satan caused.

1. First Trumpet (Rev 8:7)

> [7]*The first angel sounded: And hail and fire followed, mingled with blood, and they were thrown to the earth. And a third of the trees were burned up, and all green grass was burned up.*

A third of earth's vegetation will be destroyed with hail and fire with blood.

- Ez 38:22: "And I will bring him to judgment with pestilence and bloodshed; I will rain down on him, on his troops, and on the many peoples who are with him, flooding rain, great hailstones, fire, and brimstone."

2. Second Trumpet (Rev 8:8–9)

> [8]*Then the second angel sounded: And something like a great mountain burning with fire was thrown into the sea, and a third of the sea became blood.* [9]*And a third of the living creatures in the sea died, and a third of the ships were destroyed.*

A third of the sea creatures die, and a third of the ships are destroyed.

- Ez 14:19: "'Or if I send a pestilence into that land and pour out My fury on it in blood, and cut off from it man and beast, even though Noah, Daniel, and Job were in it, as I live,' says the Lord God, 'they would deliver neither son nor daughter; they would deliver only themselves by their righteousness.'"

3. Third Trumpet (Rev 8:10–11)

> [10]*Then the third angel sounded: And a great star fell from heaven, burning like a torch, and it fell on a third of the rivers and on the springs of water.* [11]*The name of the star is Wormwood. A third of the waters became wormwood, and many men died from the water, because it was made bitter.*

A third of the fresh water rivers will become contaminated.

- Jer 9:13–16: "And the LORD said, 'Because they have forsaken My law which I set before them, and have not obeyed My voice, nor walked according to it, but they have walked according to the dictates of their own hearts and after the Baals, which their fathers taught them,' therefore thus says the LORD of hosts, the God of Israel: 'Behold, I will feed them, this people, with wormwood, and give them water of gall to drink. I will scatter them also among the Gentiles, whom neither they nor their fathers have known. And I will send a sword after them until I have consumed them.'"
- La 3:9–19: "He has blocked my ways with hewn stone; He has made my paths crooked. He has been to me a bear lying in wait, like a lion in ambush. He has turned aside my ways and torn me in pieces; He has made me desolate. He has bent His bow and set me up as a target for the arrow. He has caused the arrows of His quiver to pierce my loins. I have become the ridicule of all my people—Their taunting song all the day. He has filled me with bitterness, He has made me drink wormwood. He has also broken my teeth with gravel, and covered me with ashes. You have moved my soul far from peace; I have forgotten prosperity. And I said, 'My strength and my hope have perished from the LORD.' Remember my affliction and roaming, the wormwood and the gall."

Both Scriptures above from Jeremiah speak of Israel's judgment because they have forsaken the Lord. It describes wormwood as water with gall in it. Gall is a bitter, greenish fluid secreted by the liver—bile. It is something bitter or distasteful, a bitter feeling.

4. Fourth Trumpet (Rev 8:12–13)

> *[12]Then the fourth angel sounded: And a third of the sun was struck, a third of the moon, and a third of the stars, so that a third of them were darkened. A third of the day did not shine, and likewise the night. [13]And I looked, and I heard an angel flying through the midst of heaven, saying with a loud voice, "Woe, woe, woe to the inhabitants of the earth, because of the remaining blasts of the trumpet of the three angels who are about to sound!"*

A third of the sun, moon, and stars will be darkened, and the day will not shine for a third part of the day.

- Lk 21:25–28: "And there will be signs in the sun, in the moon, and in the stars; and on the earth distress of nations, with perplexity, the sea and the waves roaring; men's hearts failing them from fear and the expectation of those things which are coming on the earth, for the powers of the heavens will be shaken. Then they will see the Son of Man coming in a cloud with power and great glory. Now when these things begin to happen, look up and lift up your heads, because your redemption draws near."

5. Fifth Trumpet (Rev 9:1–12)

There are three woes in the fifth, sixth, and seventh trumpets that become exceedingly worsened as they progress.

> *[1]Then the fifth angel sounded: And I saw a star fallen from heaven to the earth. To him was given the key to the bottomless pit. [2]And he opened the bottomless pit, and smoke arose out of the pit like the smoke of a great furnace. So the sun and the air were darkened because of the smoke of the pit.*

- Jdg 7:12: "Now the Midianites and Amalekites, all the people of the East, were lying in the valley as numerous as locusts; and their camels were without number, as the sand by the seashore in multitude."
- Jer 8:3: "'Then death shall be chosen rather than life by all the residue of those who remain of this evil family, who remain in all the places where I have driven them,' says the Lord of hosts."
- Joel 1:6: "For a nation has come up against My land, strong and without number; His teeth and the teeth of a lion, and he has the fangs of a fierce lion."
- Joel 2:5–7: "With a noise like chariots over mountaintops they leap, like the noise of a flaming fire that devours the stubble, like a strong people set in battle array. Before them the people writhe in pain; all faces are drained of color. They run like mighty men, they climb the wall like men of war; every one marches in formation, and they do not break ranks."

<u>Woe 1:</u> demon locusts will inflict those with the mark of the Beast for five months.

> *3Then out of the smoke locusts came upon the earth. And to them was given power, as the scorpions of the earth have power. 4They were commanded not to harm the grass of the earth, or any green thing, or any tree, but only those men who do not have the seal of God on their foreheads. 5And they were not given authority to kill them, but to torment them for five months. Their torment was like the torment of a scorpion when it strikes a man. 6In those days men will seek death and will not find it; they will desire to die, and death will flee from them. 7The shape of the locusts was like horses prepared for battle. On their heads were crowns of something like gold, and their faces were like the faces of men. 8They had hair like women's hair, and their teeth were like lions' teeth. 9And they had breastplates like breastplates of iron, and the sound of their wings was like the sound of chariots with many horses running into battle.*

> [10]*They had tails like scorpions, and there were stings in their tails. Their power was to hurt men five months.*

Here again we have spirits like horses. They have been given power from God for five months.

> [11]*And they had as king over them the angel of the bottomless pit, whose name in Hebrew is Abaddon, but in Greek he has the name Apollyon.* [12]*One woe is past. Behold, still two more woes are coming after these things.*

The word king here is ruler. There has been a ruler over these demons in the bottomless pit where they have probably been confined since Satan and his fallen angels were sent out of heaven.

6. Sixth Trumpet (Rev 9:13–21)

> [13]*Then the sixth angel sounded: And I heard a voice from the four horns of the golden altar which is before God,* [14]*saying to the sixth angel who had the trumpet, "Release the four angels who are bound at the great river Euphrates."* [15]*So the four angels, who had been prepared for the hour and day and month and year, were released to kill a third of mankind.* [16]*Now the number of the army of the horsemen was two hundred million; I heard the number of them.* [17]*And thus I saw the horses in the vision: those who sat on them had breastplates of fiery red, hyacinth blue, and sulfur yellow; and the heads of the horses were like the heads of lions; and out of their mouths came fire, smoke, and brimstone.* [18]*By these three plagues a third of mankind was killed—by the fire and the smoke and the brimstone which came out of their mouths.* [19]*For their power is in their mouth and in their tails; for their tails are like serpents, having heads; and with them they do harm.* [20]*But the rest of mankind, who were not killed by these plagues, did not repent of the works of their hands, that they should not worship demons, and idols of*

gold, silver, brass, stone, and wood, which can neither see nor hear nor walk. [21]And they did not repent of their murders or their sorceries or their sexual immorality or their thefts.

Woe 2: a third of humanity will be slain by an army of two hundred million, yet they will not repent. How many times have we heard that the Euphrates River has to dry up so that only China can send an army of two hundred million? Notice that this army consists of demon angels. This is not the work of humanity but of God. All the plagues in Egypt were brought about by God. The Euphrates dried up over the last five months while humanity was being inflicted with locusts. The Euphrates is where the city of Babylon is and is the headquarters for Satan. The people find themselves parched and cannot find water, only fire, smoke and brimstone. Only after five months, after the demon locusts are finished, does Jesus order that two hundred million demons be released from the abyss now to kill, not torment.

- Is 5:28–29: "Whose arrows are sharp, and all their bows bend; their horses' hooves will seem like flint, and their wheels like a whirlwind. Their roaring will be like a lion, they will roar like young lions; yes, they will roar and lay hold of the prey; they will carry it away safely, and no one will deliver."
- Ez 38:4: "I will turn you around, put hooks into your jaws, and lead you out, with all your army, horses, and horsemen, all splendidly clothed, a great company with bucklers and shields, all of them handling swords."
- Da 5:23: "And you have lifted yourself up against the Lord of heaven. They have brought the vessels of His house before you, and you and your lords, your wives and your concubines, have drunk wine with them. And you have praised the gods of silver and gold, bronze and iron, wood and stone, which do not see or hear or know; and the God who holds your breath in His hand and owns all your ways, you have not glorified."
- 1Co 10:20: "Rather, that the things which the Gentiles sacrifice they sacrifice to demons and not to God, and I do not want you to have fellowship with demons."

I said that the U.S. Census had 6,852,472,823 when I did the analysis of those dying in the seal judgments. If you subtract the 1,713,118,206, you get 5,139,354,617 to face this second round of trumpet judgments. A third of this population is 1,713,118,206, leaving 3,426,236,411. Of course, this does not subtract those who entered heaven through grace in the rapture. God is talking about wiping out half the population during each of the first two judgments. Maybe three billion lost people will go through the last set of judgments. This will be the biggest death toll ever.

Second Judgment—Judgment of Jews (Rev 10:1–7)

> [1]*I saw still another mighty angel* [Christ] *coming down from heaven, clothed with a cloud. And a rainbow was on his head; his face was like the sun, and his feet like pillars of fire.* [2]*He had a little book open in his hand. And he set his right foot on the sea and his left foot on the land,* [over all the earth] [3]*and cried with a loud voice, as when a lion roars. When he cried out, seven thunders uttered their voices.* [4]*Now when the seven thunders uttered their voices, I was about to write; but I heard a voice from heaven saying to me, "Seal up the things which the seven thunders uttered, and do not write them."* [5]*The angel whom I saw standing on the sea and on the land raised up his hand to heaven* [6]*and swore by Him who lives forever and ever, who created heaven and the things that are in it, the earth and the things that are in it, and the sea and the things that are in it, that there should be delay no longer,* [7]*but in the days of the sounding of the seventh angel, when he is about to sound, the mystery of God would be finished, as He declared to His servants the prophets.*

This mighty angel coming down from heaven is described as Christ seen in 1:12–16. Christ is also described in 5:5 as the Lion of the Tribe of Judah. When Christ places His feet on the earth, He is ready to take possession of His inheritance. There will be no longer a delay in the battle with Satan.

- Da 12:4–9: "'But you, Daniel, shut up the words, and seal the book until the time of the end; many shall run to and fro, and knowledge shall increase.' Then I, Daniel, looked; and there stood two others, one on the riverbank and the other on that riverbank. And one said to the man clothed in linen, who was above the waters of the river, 'How long shall the fulfillment of these wonders be?' Then I heard the man clothed in linen, who was above the waters of the river, when he held up his right hand and his left hand to heaven, and swore by Him who lives forever, that it shall be for a time, times, and half a time; and when the power of the holy people has been completely shattered, all these things shall be finished. Although I heard, I did not understand. Then I said, 'My Lord, what shall be the end of these things?' And he said, 'Go your way, Daniel, for the words are closed up and sealed till the time of the end.'"

John Ate the Little Book (Rev 10:8–11)

> *[8]Then the voice which I heard from heaven spoke to me again and said, "Go, take the little book which is open in the hand of the angel who stands on the sea and on the earth." [9]So I went to the angel and said to him, "Give me the little book." And he said to me, "Take and eat it; and it will make your stomach bitter, but it will be as sweet as honey in your mouth." [10]Then I took the little book out of the angel's hand and ate it, and it was as sweet as honey in my mouth. But when I had eaten it, my stomach became bitter. [11]And he said to me, "You must prophesy again about many peoples, nations, tongues, and kings."*

Christ is ready in the next chapter to reveal the mystery of God to allow Satan to be the prince of the power of the air on the earth these six thousand years. Could this book be the Holy Book, the Word of God completed in the fullness of God? It was God's plan to endure the bitter until the sweet came. Now is the celebration of the King. All the prophecies have been fulfilled.

- Jer 15:16: "Your words were found, and I ate them, and Your word was to me the joy and rejoicing of my heart; for I am called by Your name, O Lord God of hosts."

- Ez 2:9–10: "Now when I looked, there was a hand stretched out to me; and behold, a scroll of a book was in it. Then He spread it before me; and there was writing on the inside and on the outside, and written on it were lamentations and mourning and woe."

The Two Witnesses (Rev 11:1–6)

> [1]*Then I was given a reed like a measuring rod. And the angel stood, saying, "Rise and measure the temple of God, the altar, and those who worship there.* [2]*But leave out the court which is outside the temple, and do not measure it, for it has been given to the Gentiles. And they will tread the holy city underfoot for forty-two months.*

This is one place in the Bible where we know the Jewish calendar was based on the lunar year of thirty days per month. Forty-two months in verse 2 is the same as 1,260 days in verse 3, three and a half years. We are definitely at midpoint in the tribulation—forty-two months or 1,260 days are left.

This same angel who told John to eat the book is now telling him to measure the newly erected temple in Jerusalem, the place of the presence of God with His people. The rebuilding of the temple was prophesied in Daniel 9:27. John is also told to measure the altar, which is where the sacrificial system will be reinstated during the millennium. He was to leave out the court as that was for the Gentiles and the times of the Gentiles is over (Lk 21:24).

> [3]*And I will give power to my two witnesses, and they will prophesy one thousand two hundred and sixty days, clothed in sackcloth."*

Neither Enoch nor Elijah died, and according to Hebrews 9:27, everyone must die. Deuteronomy 17:6 and 19:15 call for two witnesses. These witnesses have been preaching during the first three and a half years of the tribulation. They will be protected to tell the truth—the Messiah came as Jesus Christ, and what is happening is written in the Word of God.

Matthew 24:14 says that the gospel of the kingdom will be preached in all the world for a witness unto all nations.

- Heb 9:27: "It is appointed for men to die once, but after this the judgment."

> *[4]These are the two olive trees and the two lampstands standing before the God of the earth. [5]And if anyone wants to harm them, fire proceeds from their mouth and devours their enemies. And if anyone wants to harm them, he must be killed in this manner. [6]These have power to shut heaven, so that no rain falls in the days of their prophecy; and they have power over waters to turn them to blood, and to strike the earth with all plagues, as often as they desire.*

The two witnesses are compared to two olive trees and two lampstands prophesied in Zechariah 4. We know the olive oil is the Holy Spirit and the lampstands bear the truth of the Word of God. Zechariah 4:14 says, "These are the two anointed ones, who stand beside the Lord of the whole earth."

- 1Ki 17:1: "And Elijah the Tishbite, of the inhabitants of Gilead, said to Ahab, 'As the Lord God of Israel lives, before whom I stand, there shall not be dew nor rain these years, except at my word.'"
- 2Ki 1:10: "So Elijah answered and said to the captain of fifty, 'If I am a man of God, then let fire come down from heaven and consume you and your fifty men.' And fire came down from heaven and consumed him and his fifty."

The Witnesses Killed (Rev 11:7–10)

> *[7]When they finish their testimony, the beast that ascends out of the bottomless pit will make war against them, overcome them, and kill them. [8]And their dead bodies will lie in the street of the great city which spiritually is called Sodom and Egypt, where also our Lord was crucified. [9]Then those from the*

> *peoples, tribes, tongues, and nations will see their dead bodies three-and-a-half days, and not allow their dead bodies to be put into graves. [10]And those who dwell on the earth will rejoice over them, make merry, and send gifts to one another, because these two prophets tormented those who dwell on the earth.*

When God's mission of the two witnesses is complete, the Antichrist will kill them. Satan thought that after He had Christ crucified, he had won—until Christ took away the keys to the kingdom. In fact, His crucifixion gave humanity authority over Satan in Christ's name. Now again, Satan thinks that because he killed God's men and leaves them there for the world to see that he is in charge—but God never intended for Satan to win.

- Da 7:21: "I was watching; and the same horn was making war against the saints and prevailing against them, until the Ancient of Days came and a judgment was made in favor of the saints of the Most High, and the time came for the saints to possess the kingdom."

The Witnesses Resurrected (Rev 11:11–14)

> *[11]Now after the three-and-a-half days the breath of life from God entered them, and they stood on their feet, and great fear fell on those who saw them. [12]And they heard a loud voice from heaven saying to them, "Come up here." And they ascended to heaven in a cloud, and their enemies saw them. [13]In the same hour there was a great earthquake, and a tenth of the city fell. In the earthquake seven thousand people were killed, and the rest were afraid and gave glory to the God of heaven. [14]The second woe is past. Behold, the third woe is coming quickly.*

After three days (the time Jesus was in hell taking over the keys to the kingdom after His crucifixion), the witnesses will come alive. This will be televised all over the world. They will ascend into heaven in a cloud just as Jesus did.

Woe 3: Just as with Jesus, we see an earthquake, a tenth of Jerusalem falls, and seven thousand people are killed.

7. Seventh Trumpet (Rev 11:15–19)

> *15Then the seventh angel sounded: And there were loud voices in heaven, saying, "The kingdoms of this world have become the kingdoms of our Lord and of His Christ, and He shall reign forever and ever!" 16And the twenty-four elders who sat before God on their thrones fell on their faces and worshiped God, 17saying: " We give You thanks, O Lord God Almighty, The One who is and who was and who is to come, Because You have taken Your great power and reigned. 18The nations were angry, and Your wrath has come, And the time of the dead, that they should be judged, And that You should reward Your servants the prophets and the saints, And those who fear Your name, small and great, And should destroy those who destroy the earth." 19Then the temple of God was opened in heaven, and the ark of His covenant was seen in His temple. And there were lightnings, noises, thunderings, an earthquake, and great hail.*

A holy celebration is happening because God kept His covenant with His people. God will protect His people, Israel, in the wilderness and allow the judgment now to fall upon the Gentiles who are left. These Gentiles will be judged along with Satan for coming against Israel.

CHAPTER 6

Revelation 12–13: The Great Tribulation (Characters)

Now we enter the second half of the tribulation which is described as the great tribulation.

- Chapters 12–13: Seven characters will fight until the Battle of Armageddon is won by Christ and Satan is defeated and placed in the bottomless pit.
- Chapters 14–15: God's plan is enacted with seven angels proclaiming the victory of King Jesus.
- Chapter 16: The seven bowl judgments are poured out.
- Chapters 17–19 bring forth the second advent, when Christ comes to earth to rule and reign and brings His saints with Him.

Chapters 12 and 13 are informational and show the battle of darkness against light from the beginning of time. John saw signs that symbolize the seven characters that are fighting. This is a spiritual war:

1. The Sun-Clothed Woman: The nation of Israel (Rev 12:1-2).
2. The Dragon: Satan (Anti-God) has always been the adversary of God from the beginning of time (Rev 12:3-4).
3. The Man-Child: Christ came to overcome this adversary who Satan has always been ready to devour (Rev 12:5-6).
4. The Archangel: Michael cast Satan out of heaven, which enraged him (Rev 12:7-12).

5. The Remnant: the Jewish people. Satan tried to devour the 144,000, but when he could not do so, he made war on all those who believed in Jesus Christ (Rev 12:13-17).
6. The Beast Out of the Sea: political leader (Antichrist) for Satan (Rev 13:1-10).
7. The Beast Out of the Earth: the False Prophet or religious leader (the Antispirit) for Satan (Rev 13:11-18).

1. The Sun-Clothed Woman (Rev 12:1–2)

> *1Now a great sign appeared in heaven: a woman clothed with the sun, with the moon under her feet, and on her head a garland of twelve stars. 2Then being with child, she cried out in labor and in pain to give birth.*

To view this chronologically, we go back to the beginning of time. We have switched from the story of Jesus as Lord in chapters 1–11, and now we are going to hear about the story of Satan as adversary in chapters 12 and 13. In verse 1, the woman Satan (the dragon) persecutes is the nation of Israel seen in the twelve tribes or stars. Satan was thrown from the 3rd heaven to earth at the time of his original sin (Isa 14, Ez 28). Satan continued to have access to the throne as the accuser of the brethren. Now in verse 4, Satan and his angels are sent to earth from the 2nd heaven where he has been battling a spiritual war.

- Isa 26:17: "As a woman with child is in pain and cries out in her pangs, when she draws near the time of her delivery, so have we been in Your sight, O Lord."
- Isa 66:6–9: "'The sound of noise from the city! A voice from the Temple! The voice of the Lord who fully repays His enemies! Before she was in labor, she gave birth; before her pain came, she delivered a male child. Who has heard such a thing? Who has seen such things? Shall the earth be made to give birth in one day? Or shall a nation be born at once? For as soon as Zion was in labor, she gave birth to her children. Shall I bring to the time of birth, and not cause delivery?' Says the Lord."

2. The Dragon (Rev 12:3–4)

> [3a]*And another sign [symbol] appeared in heaven: behold, a great, fiery red dragon having seven heads and ten horns, and seven diadems on his heads.*

The seven heads represent seven consecutive evil world empires controlled by Satan that ends with the revival of the Roman Empire. They are Egypt, Assyria, Babylon, Medo-Persia, Greece, Rome, and finally the revised Roman Empire. Daniel 7 refers to this revived Roman Empire that will be known as the European Union (EU). The little horn (Antichrist or the fiery red dragon) comes out of the ten horns (nations of the EU). The seven diadems will be seven leaders to be formed from the original ten EU nations.

> [3b]*And the dragon stood before the woman who was ready to give birth, to devour her Child as soon as it was born.*

When Jesus was born, Satan was always ready to devour Him.

> [4]*His tail drew a third of the stars of heaven and threw them to the earth.*

The stars of heaven attached to his tail reveal the fact that Satan will take with him in his expulsion from heaven a third of the angels who have become sinful because they worship their lord Satan. Angels are spoken of as stars in the Old Testament (Job 38:7).

3. The Man-Child (Rev 12:5)

> [5]*She bore a male Child who was to rule all nations with a rod of iron. And her Child was caught up to God and His throne. Then the woman fled into the wilderness, where she has a place prepared by God, that they should feed her there one thousand two hundred and sixty days.*

Jesus, the Christ child, the Messiah, ruined Satan's plans when He was snatched by God to the throne. Now, after Satan has been thrown from heaven, God will protect His people, the Israelites, by taking them into the wilderness (actually happens in 14:1–7) to escape the Antichrist. Ruling with an iron rod will be a theocratic rule totally under the supreme control of the Lord. According to the Bible, this means He will rule in love. It won't be about the government governing but each governing to show themselves approved to almighty God for His grace accorded to them.

- Mt 2:16: "Then Herod, when he saw that he was deceived by the wise men, was exceedingly angry; and he sent forth and put to death all the male children who were in Bethlehem and in all its districts, from two years old and under, according to the time which he had determined from the wise men."
- Acts 1:9–11: "Now when He had spoken these things, while they watched, He was taken up, and a cloud received Him out of their sight. And while they looked steadfastly toward heaven as He went up, behold, two men stood by them in white apparel, who also said, 'Men of Galilee, why do you stand gazing up into heaven? This same Jesus, who was taken up from you into heaven, will so come in like manner as you saw Him go into heaven.'"

4. The Archangel (Rev 12:7-12)

> *7And war broke out in heaven: Michael and his angels fought with the dragon; and the dragon and his angels fought, 8but they did not prevail, nor was a place found for them in heaven any longer. 9So the great dragon was cast out, that serpent of old, called the Devil and Satan, who deceives the whole world; he was cast to the earth, and his angels were cast out with him. 10Then I heard a loud voice saying in heaven, "Now salvation, and strength, and the kingdom of our God, and the power of His Christ have come, for the accuser of our brethren, who accused them before our God day and night, has been cast down. 11And*

> *they overcame him by the blood of the Lamb and by the word of their testimony, and they did not love their lives to the death.* [12]*Therefore rejoice, O heavens, and you who dwell in them! Woe to the inhabitants of the earth and the sea! For the devil has come down to you, having great wrath, because he knows that he has a short time."*

This verse explains how Satan was expelled from the heavenlies. Ezekiel prophesied that Satan was originally cast out of heaven (Ez 28:17–18), and when he continued to sin, God destroyed the earth that God made perfect (Ps 18:30). In order for God to be righteous, He cannot tolerate sin. Because He is holy and good, God must deal with sin and its originator, Satan.

Satan is expressed in the Bible as the god of this age (2Co 4:4) and the prince of the power of the air (Eph 2:2). Satan is the king of the kingdom of darkness. His kingdom is described in Ephesians 6:12 as principalities, powers, the rulers of the darkness of this age, and spiritual hosts of wickedness in the heavenly places. The Lord God has allowed him to test each human so they would choose God and His righteousness over the corruption of Satan. God created Satan just as He did every other spirit. And though God allowed Satan to rule the world systems, 1 Corinthians 10:26 says the earth and the fullness thereof is the Lord's.

- Ro 16:20: "And the God of peace will crush Satan under your feet shortly. The grace of our Lord Jesus Christ be with you. Amen."

5. The Remnant (Rev 12:5)

> [13]*Now when the dragon saw that he had been cast to the earth, he persecuted the woman who gave birth to the male Child.* [14]*But the woman was given two wings of a great eagle, that she might fly into the wilderness to her place, where she is nourished for a time and times and half a time, from the presence of the serpent.*

The expulsion from the heavenlies must have been a superior victory for Michael; Satan knew that he was defeated and that the heavenlies were cleansed of all darkness. Satan's venom was unleashed on the woman Israel and he knows this is his last chance to take out as many as he can.

The eagle's wings speak of the swiftness of Israel to be safely delivered into the wilderness just as God protected Israel when they fled from the Egyptians in Exodus 19.

During the second half of the tribulation, God will nourish any who turn to him as He did for those who escaped into the wilderness for forty years under the leadership of Moses. When God poured out the plagues in Egypt, the Israelites did not experience them in the land of Goshen. God very conveniently placed them far enough from the city in which Pharaoh lived. There will be many people preserved upon earth to live through the millennium.

- Isa 59:19: "So shall they fear the name of the LORD from the west, and His glory from the rising of the sun; when the enemy comes in like a flood, the Spirit of the LORD will lift up a standard against him."

> [15]*So the serpent spewed water out of his mouth like a flood after the woman, that he might cause her to be carried away by the flood.* [16]*But the earth helped the woman, and the earth opened its mouth and swallowed up the flood which the dragon had spewed out of his mouth.* [17]*And the dragon was enraged with the woman, and he went to make war with the rest of her offspring, who keep the commandments of God and have the testimony of Jesus Christ.*

It is believed that when the Israelites escape, they will go to the ancient city of Petra across the Jordan River. Satan will somehow create a flood to destroy it, but God will cause the earth to open up and swallow up this flood.

6. The Beast out of the Sea (Rev 13:1–10)

> [1]*Then I stood on the sand of the sea. And I saw a beast rising up out of the sea, having seven heads and ten horns, and on*

his horns ten crowns, and on his heads a blasphemous name. [2]Now the beast which I saw was like a leopard, his feet were like the feet of a bear, and his mouth like the mouth of a lion. The dragon gave him his power, his throne, and great authority.

The beast out of the sea is the political leader, or Antichrist. After the dragon (Satan) is cast out of heaven, the Beast appears. Satan, the dragon, was sent from the third heaven when he threatened to take God's throne as told in Isaiah 14 and Ezekiel 28. Now, Satan and his angels are being thrown from the second heaven, where the spiritual wars are fought. He has just lost his spiritual foothold and is extremely angry. So where does he go? He incarnates himself into the Antichrist. It is now that the Antichrist breaks his covenant with Israel, stands up in the temple, and says "I am God," and his eternal desire is that everyone would worship him, Satan.

He further brags of how up until now, Satan has disguised himself, but now he comes out of hiding. He was the Beast Daniel saw. He admits he ruled over the seven evil kingdoms and now is dictator over the world through the ten leaders he controls. The Lord allows him to rule and reign for the second half of the tribulation so all those who are destined for eternal life with Jesus can make this decision. Daniel 11:37 says that the Antichrist will place himself above all gods. Islam will not accept any other religion than that of Muhammad.

The four beasts are the four kingdoms or Gentile world powers we saw in Daniel 2 in Nebuchadnezzar's dream. God shared with Nebuchadnezzar, a Gentile and enemy of Israel, the prophetic vision of the latter days. This was the vision of the Gentile empires to rule: a statue stood before Nebuchadnezzar with a head of gold, chest and arms of silver, belly and thighs of bronze, and legs of iron and clay.

- Da 7:2–7: "Daniel spoke, saying, 'I saw in my vision by night, and behold, the four winds of heaven were stirring up the Great Sea. And four great beasts came up from the sea, each different from the other. The first was like a lion, and had eagle's wings. I watched till its wings were plucked off; and it was lifted up from the earth and made to stand on two feet like a man, and a man's heart was

> given to it. And suddenly another beast, a second, like a bear. It was raised up on one side, and had three ribs in its mouth between its teeth. And they said thus to it: "Arise, devour much flesh!" After this I looked, and there was another, like a leopard, which had on its back four wings of a bird. The beast also had four heads, and dominion was given to it. After this I saw in the night visions, and behold, a fourth beast, dreadful and terrible, exceedingly strong. It had huge iron teeth; it was devouring, breaking in pieces, and trampling the residue with its feet. It was different from all the beasts that were before it, and it had ten horns.'"

The interpretation is that there will be four world empires to rule over Israel from his reign until the forthcoming reign of the Messiah.

- 586–539 BC: Nebuchadnezzar, the Babylonian Empire (gold)
- 538–332 BC: Darius the Mede and Cyrus the Person, the Medo-Persian Empire (silver)
- 332–63 BC: Alexander the Great, the Grecian Empire (bronze)
- 63 BC: Pompey, the Roman Empire (iron and clay)

Metal	Kingdom	Beast	Description
Gold	Babylon	Lion	Strongest—the lion is the king of the beasts; a lion with wings suggests strength and swiftness.
Silver	Medo-Persia	Bear	Two nations fought, but one raised itself up higher than the other; Cyrus was king of Persia. The bear symbolized large armies moving slow but mightily with massive destruction. The three ribs are the skeletal remains of the last three provinces: Egypt, Lydia, and Babylon, which are captured.

Metal	Kingdom	Beast	Description
Bronze	Greece	Leopard	The leopard is Alexander the Great, swift and powerful; reigning only ten years. Xerxes' expedition against Greece was undertaken with 2,500,000 fighting men. The four heads are the four generals who succeed and are Cassander; Seleucus; Lysimachus, and Ptolemy. Antiochus Epiphanes IV desecrated the temple.
Iron and Clay	Rome	Iron Teeth	Rome was known for its use of iron in its weapons during the fourth world empire. Nero and Domitian devoured their enemies and broke them into pieces. They burned the temple in Jerusalem in AD 70.
10 Horns	1 World Order	10 Nations	Still future. Perhaps the European Union; there may be many nations; there will be ten major nations.
Little Horn	Antichrist	1 World Ruler	Still future (tribulation in the book of Revelation). He will destroy three other major nations in order to reign.

There is a beast out of the sea and a beast out of the earth. The Beast out of the sea is the Antichrist, a political leader who will rule over the revised Roman Empire. The beast out of the earth is a religious leader called the False Prophet, who will lead worship of the political leader, the Antichrist. The ten horns are the leaders of the ten nations in the revised Roman Empire. Out of the ten comes the little horn (the Antichrist), who puts down three of the rulers and then dominates the other seven.

> [3]*And I saw one of his heads as if it had been mortally wounded, and his deadly wound was healed. And all the world marveled*

> *and followed the beast. [4]So they worshiped the dragon who gave authority to the beast; and they worshiped the beast, saying, "Who is like the beast? Who is able to make war with him?" [5]And he was given a mouth speaking great things and blasphemies, and he was given authority to continue for forty-two months. [6]Then he opened his mouth in blasphemy against God, to blaspheme His name, His tabernacle, and those who dwell in heaven. [7]It was granted to him to make war with the saints and to overcome them. And authority was given him over every tribe, tongue, and nation. [8]All who dwell on the earth will worship him, whose names have not been written in the Book of Life of the Lamb slain from the foundation of the world. [9]If anyone has an ear, let him hear. [10]He who leads into captivity shall go into captivity; he who kills with the sword must be killed with the sword. Here is the patience and the faith of the saints.*

The Antichrist is mortally wounded and miraculously healed, which is a counterfeit resurrection. This enables the Antichrist to be looked upon as the supernatural world leader. Verse 5 shows that we are at the midpoint in the tribulation because he has authority for forty-two months.

Larkin[4] helps us understand these world powers, "While these four great empires were to follow each other in order, they were not to follow without a break. The Roman Empire lasted until 364 AD when it was divided into its eastern and western divisions. Since then there has been no leading world empire, and cannot be according to this prophecy until Christ sets up His stone or Millennial Kingdom, as represented by the stone that smites the colossus (image) on its feet, for this Stone Kingdom is to fill the whole earth, and thus be universal. This stone cannot be Christianity, for it does not fill the earth by degrees, and thus crowd out the Colossus, but it at one blow demolishes it. The action of the stone is that of judgment, not grace, and is sudden and calamitous. Again the time of the destruction is not until after the formation of the toes, and we know that the two limbs did not appear until 364 AD, and the ten toes have not yet developed. The time when the stone falls on the feet we are told is in the days of those kings (Da 2:44), that is the kings represented by the ten toes, which as we shall see corresponds with the ten horns of Daniel's fourth wild beast (Da 7:7-8) and with the ten kings of John's beast (Rev 17:12). The first four kingdoms were literal kingdoms, and so must the Stone Kingdom be, for it is to take the place of those kingdoms and fill the whole earth. It represents therefore the Millennial Kingdom of Christ for He is the Stone of the Scriptures (Mt 21:44).

"From what we have thus far learned of the Antichrist, the probability is that he will be a Syrian Jew (Is 52), for it is not likely that the Jews will accept as their Messiah one who is not a Jew, unless the claimant by false pretense makes them believe he is one. This, however, does not prevent the Antichrist from being a Roman citizen, and the political head of the revived Roman Empire, for Saul of Tarsus was both a Jew and a Roman citizen."

- Da 2:28–35: "But there is a God in heaven who reveals secrets, and He has made known to King Nebuchadnezzar what will be in the latter days. Your dream, and the visions of your head upon your bed, were these: As for you, O king, thoughts came to your mind while on your bed, about what would come to pass after this; and He who reveals secrets has made known to you what will be. But as for me, this secret has not been revealed to me because I have more wisdom than anyone living, but for our sakes who make known the interpretation to the king, and that you may know the thoughts of your heart. You, O king, were watching; and behold, a great image! This great image, whose splendor was excellent, stood before you; and its form was awesome. This image's head was of fine gold, its chest and arms of silver, its belly and thighs of bronze, its legs of iron, its feet partly of iron and partly of clay. You watched while a stone was cut out without hands, which struck the image on its feet of iron and clay, and broke them in pieces. Then the iron, the clay, the bronze, the silver, and the gold were crushed together, and became like chaff from the summer threshing floors; the wind carried them away so that no trace of them was found. And the stone that struck the image became a great mountain and filled the whole earth."

- Da 7:21–25: "I was watching; and the same horn was making war against the saints, and prevailing against them, until the Ancient of Days came, and a judgment was made in favor of the saints of the Most High, and the time came for the saints to possess the kingdom. Thus he said: 'The fourth beast shall be a fourth kingdom on earth, which shall be different from all other kingdoms, and shall devour the whole earth, Trample it and break it in pieces. The ten horns are ten kings who shall arise from this kingdom. And another shall rise after them; he shall be different from the first ones, and shall subdue three kings. He shall speak pompous words against the Most High, shall persecute the saints of the Most High, and shall intend to change times and law. Then the saints shall be given into his hand For a time and times and half a time.'"

As the little horn of Daniel's fourth wild beast, the Antichrist will destroy three of the ten kings and firmly establish himself in the place of power. As the little horn does not appear until after the ten horns or ten federated kingdoms come into existence, it is clear that the Antichrist does not form the federation but comes out of it.

7. The Beast out of the Earth (Rev 13:11–18)

> *11Then I saw another beast coming up out of the earth, and he had two horns like a lamb and spoke like a dragon. 12And he exercises all the authority of the first beast in his presence, and causes the earth and those who dwell in it to worship the first beast, whose deadly wound was healed. 13He performs great signs, so that he even makes fire come down from heaven on the earth in the sight of men. 14And he deceives those who dwell on the earth by those signs which he was granted to do in the sight of the beast, telling those who dwell on the earth to make an image to the beast who was wounded by the sword and lived. 15He was granted power to give breath to the image of the beast, that the image of the beast should both speak and cause as many as would not worship the image of the beast to be killed. 16He*

> *causes all, both small and great, rich and poor, free and slave, to receive a mark on their right hand or on their foreheads, [17]and that no one may buy or sell except one who has the mark or the name of the beast, or the number of his name. [18]Here is wisdom. Let him who has understanding calculate the number of the beast, for it is the number of a man: His number is 666.*

This beast is not the Antichrist but the False Prophet (the Antispirit) or religious leader.

- 2Th 2:9: "The coming of the lawless one is according to the working of Satan, with all power, signs, and lying wonders."

The number 7 is used in Revelation to represent the fullness of Christ that has finally come about. The number 6 is the number of mankind. The Antichrist is an imitator, so the 666 is likely his representation of the fullness of humanity in the world system. The false trinity is Satan as God, the Antichrist as the false Christ, and the False Prophet as the false Holy Spirit. Satan has many demons today that give us thoughts that are lies. Here, this image will have power to speak audibly, which those with demon possession have the power to do today. Satan will give this image a demonic spirit to speak. All will be commanded to worship the image or be put to death, much like the image that Nebuchadnezzar commanded to be worshiped in Daniel 3.

CHAPTER 7

Revelation 14–15: Christ with the Tribulation Saints

Seven Angels Proclaim the Victory of King Jesus

First, the Lamb comes to claim the nation of Israel. Then He dispatches His angels. Below is the sequence of events in Revelation 14 and 15.

1. Lamb Raptures Israel (Rev 14:1-7)
   The first angel **proclaims** that the hour of judgment has come. It is no longer near as was proclaimed by Christ in the Gospels
2. Babylon will Fall (Rev 14:8)
   The second angel **proclaims** that Babylon will fall and be destroyed.
3. Torment to Those Who Receive the Mark (Rev 14:9-13)
   The third angel **proclaims** that those who receive the mark will receive God's wrath (the great tribulation).
4. Harvest will be Reaped (Rev 14:14-16)
   The fourth angel **proclaims** the seven bowl judgments will be poured out.
5. Grapes will be Ripe (Rev 14:17-18)
   The fifth angel **proclaims** that the bowl judgments will climax in the Battle of Armageddon.
6. Winepress will be Trampled (Rev 14:19-20)
   The sixth angel **proclaims** that the power of fire shall destroy Satan's power.

7. God's Temple in Heaven will be Filled with Glory (Rev 15:1-8) The seventh angel **proclaims** that the blood will rise to the horses' bridles.

A proclamation in the Greek is *plerophoreo* and means to bring in full measure, to fulfill or accomplish. This is the last warning, for the hour of judgment is here. Amos 3:7 tells us that God will not do anything unless He tells us; otherwise, it is not for His glory. Isaiah 43:7 tells us that everything is for His glory. Jesus will show us the chronological details we can expect through the great tribulation. Therefore, chapters 14 and 15 are proclamations, proclaiming Jesus as King over the world. Chapter 16 shows how the bowl judgments will be released, and then in chapters 17 and 18 is the destruction of the world system that culminates in chapter 19 with the second advent of Jesus Christ. We must realize that what is being proclaimed here in chapters 14–15 is like unveiling God's plan, but it isn't enacted until future chapters. That is why Revelation doesn't look like it is chronological, though it is. Chapters 14 and 15 are prophecies.

Event	Proclaimed	Event Occurs
Lamb raptures Israel (144,000)		14:1–6
Hour of judgment has come		14:7
Babylon will fall	14:8	18
Those w/mark will receive wrath	14:9–11	20:4–6
Martyrs will be saved	14:12	20:4–6
Harvest will be reaped	14:14–15	20:4–6
Seven bowl or vial judgments poured out	14:16	16
World religious system will be destroyed		17
World government and financial system destroyed		18
Climax will be in Armageddon		19
Fire will destroy Satan's power		19
Blood will rise to horses' bridles		19
God's temple filled with glory	15	19
Marriage supper of the Lamb		19
Antichrist and Antispirit (two beasts cast into lake of fire)		19
AntiGod (Satan) bound in bottomless pit for 1,000 years		19

Israel will be taken out before the great tribulation. This is in character with the Lord. Adam, Enoch, and Methuselah died just before God brought forth the flood with Noah (Ge 5). God removed the Christians from the earth before the seal judgments (Rev 4). God removed the martyrs before the trumpet judgments (Rev 7). Now He will remove Israel before the bowl judgments. God always protects His people.

1. Lamb Raptures Israel (Rev 14:1-7)

> [1]*Then I looked, and behold, a Lamb standing on Mount Zion, and with Him one hundred and forty-four thousand, having His Father's name written on their foreheads.* [2]*And I heard a voice from heaven, like the voice of many waters, and like the voice of loud thunder. And I heard the sound of harpists playing their harps.* [3]*They sang as it were a new song before the throne, before the four living creatures, and the elders; and no one could learn that song except the hundred and forty-four thousand who were redeemed from the earth.* [4]*These are the ones who were not defiled with women, for they are virgins. These are the ones who follow the Lamb wherever He goes. These were redeemed from among men, being firstfruits to God and to the Lamb.* [5]*And in their mouth was found no deceit, for they are without fault before the throne of God.*

Jesus is coming to get Israel at the sound of the trumpet—maybe on the Feast of Trumpets during the great tribulation. They sang a new song before the throne that was never sung before because this is the firstfruits of Israel to God. Israel is finally around the throne. Can you imagine the celebration when God can bring His people Israel at last before Him?

- Joel 2:28–32: "And it shall come to pass afterward that I will pour out My Spirit on all flesh; your sons and your daughters shall prophesy, your old men shall dream dreams, your young men shall see visions. And also on My menservants and on My maidservants I will pour out My Spirit in those days. And I will show wonders in the heavens and in the earth: Blood and fire and

> pillars of smoke. The sun shall be turned into darkness, and the moon into blood, before the coming of the great and awesome day of the LORD. And it shall come to pass that whoever calls on the name of the LORD shall be saved. For in Mount Zion and in Jerusalem there shall be deliverance, as the LORD has said, among the remnant whom the LORD calls."

We now have the standoff of the dragon on the shore (12:17) and the Lion of the tribe of Judah on Mount Zion or the Temple Mount. The Dome of the Rock of Islam was the Temple Mount. The dome is over the rock the Jewish people call the foundation stone, where Abraham offered Isaac in Genesis 22, the same place where King David purchased the threshing floor from Araunah the Jebusite in 2 Samuel 24, and where Solomon built the temple in 2 Chronicles 3. This is the site where Jesus will return.

We must see this as the time when all Israel (those who turned to believe Jesus Christ is the Messiah) will be saved according to Romans 11:26. Once Israel is raptured, the great tribulation can proceed. God will always protect His people. The 144,000 consist of the 12,000 in each of the twelve tribes. This is not necessarily a head count but a total representation of Israel. When the 144,000 fled to the wilderness for protection, there were others in Jerusalem who obeyed God's commandments (Rev 12:13–17). This is when Israel is able to reign over their enemy. The text says they sang before the throne. Jesus has personally come to receive the nation of Israel into heaven to protect it before the destruction of the earth happens with the bowl or vial judgments. Israel is standing with the Lamb, its Messiah, as He brings forth judgment. Israel is being vindicated and the Messiah is allowing them to be part of this judgment against those who came against them for all time. They were saved, sealed, and kept safe to represent Israel for this moment.

> [6] *Then I saw another angel flying in the midst of heaven, having the everlasting gospel to preach to those who dwell on the earth—to every nation, tribe, tongue, and people—*[7] *saying with a loud voice, "Fear God and give glory to Him, for the hour of His judgment has come; and worship Him who made heaven and earth, the sea and springs of water."*

Since Israel is removed, the angel is now addressing every nation, all peoples left on the earth, believers and unbelievers. The everlasting gospel is the good news prophesied in the Bible. After Adam and Eve sinned, the Lord placed judgment on Satan in Genesis 3:15. He said, "And I will put enmity between you and the woman, and between your seed and her Seed; He shall bruise your head, and you shall bruise His heel." Now in Revelation, He, the Seed, is fulfilling this prophecy. He will bruise Satan's head, the promise of the Redeemer to take all authority, the head of the Serpent.

2. Babylon will Fall (Rev 14:8)

> [8]*And another angel followed, saying, "Babylon is fallen, is fallen, that great city, because she has made all nations drink of the wine of the wrath of her fornication."*

The angel is proclaiming that Babylon will fall, but we don't see that happen until Revelation 18. Babylon is the seat of Satan. We must see Babylon as a city and a system.

Zechariah 5:7–11 prophesies that in the end times a house will be built in Shinar (Iraq). Babylon was between Fallujah and Karbala between the Tigris and Euphrates Rivers in Iraq. The Antichrist will rebuild Babylon during the first half of the tribulation to include the beautiful Hanging Gardens, one of the seven wonders of the ancient world. He will begin in Rome and set up temporary headquarters while he rebuilds the temple for worship in Jerusalem and Babylon as the headquarters for his kingdom. He will not align himself with Allah of the Muslims or God of the Jews; Satan's desire has always been to be worshiped as one above the God we know. Revelation 20:4 indicates that he has anyone beheaded who does not worship him.

3. Torment to Those Who Receive the Mark (Rev 14:9–13)

> [9]*Then a third angel followed them, saying with a loud voice, "If anyone worships the beast and his image, and receives his mark on his forehead or on his hand, [10]he himself shall also drink of the*

> *wine of the wrath of God, which is poured out full strength into the cup of His indignation. He shall be tormented with fire and brimstone in the presence of the holy angels and in the presence of the Lamb. [11]And the smoke of their torment ascends forever and ever; and they have no rest day or night, who worship the beast and his image, and whoever receives the mark of his name."*

Jesus is unveiled! All heaven celebrates that the great tribulation and the final persecution by Satan is about to end: fear God and give glory to Him, for the hour of His judgment has come; and worship Him who made heaven and earth, the sea and springs of water (14:7). The Lord is now surrounded by His angels ready to deliver His wrath upon those with the mark of the Beast, for the seven bowl judgments are the promised "wrath of God." This doesn't happen until 20:4–6.

- Isa 34:8–10: "For it is the day of the LORD's vengeance, the year of recompense for the cause of Zion. Its streams shall be turned into pitch, and its dust into brimstone; its land shall become burning pitch. It shall not be quenched night or day; its smoke shall ascend forever. From generation to generation it shall lie waste; no one shall pass through it forever and ever." This describes hell that will be waiting.

> *[12]Here is the patience of the saints; here are those who keep the commandments of God and the faith of Jesus. [13]Then I heard a voice from heaven saying to me, "Write: 'Blessed are the dead who die in the Lord from now on.'" "Yes," says the Spirit, "that they may rest from their labors, and their works follow them."*

- 2Th 1:7: "And to give you who are troubled rest with us when the Lord Jesus is revealed from heaven with His mighty angels."

4. Harvest will be Reaped (Rev 14:14–16)

> *[14]Then I looked, and behold, a white cloud, and on the cloud sat One like the Son of Man, having on His head a golden crown,*

> *and in His hand a sharp sickle.* [15]*And another angel came out of the temple, crying with a loud voice to Him who sat on the cloud, "Thrust in Your sickle and reap, for the time has come for You to reap, for the harvest of the earth is ripe."* [16]*So He who sat on the cloud thrust in His sickle on the earth, and the earth was reaped.*

A warning is given to those who believe Jesus is patient; He is about to return for His harvest. The harvest is done at the sheep/goat judgment to determine those who will enter the millennial rule. This happens in chapter 19 as Jesus comes back for the Battle of Armageddon just prior to His rule. The rest of the information here describes this harvest.

"Thrust in your sickle and reap" refers to the sheep/goat judgment of those left on the earth. Matthew 13: 40-42 reads, "Therefore as the tares are gathered and burned in the fire; so will it be at the end of this age the Son of man will send out His angels, and they will gather out of his kingdom all things that offend, and those who practice lawlessness, and will cast them into a furnace of fire. There will be wailing and gnashing of teeth."

5. Grapes will be Ripe (Rev 14:17–18)

> [17]*Then another angel came out of the temple which is in heaven, he also having a sharp sickle.*

This sickle is in preparation for the Battle of Armageddon, when the harvest will be reaped.

> [18]*And another angel came out from the altar, who had power over fire, and he cried with a loud cry to him who had the sharp sickle, saying, "Thrust in your sharp sickle and gather the clusters of the vine of the earth, for her grapes are fully ripe."*

The sharp sickle will be the final judgment of vials being poured out. The harvest is fully ripe and has had a season to turn to the Lord. "Her grapes are fully ripe" conveys the thought of their being dry like raisins.

Crushed grapes make wine, which represents the blood of our Lord Jesus on His garments to indicate He has trodden the winepress.

- Joel 3:13: "Put in the sickle, for the harvest is ripe. Come, go down; for the winepress is full, the vats overflow—for their wickedness is great."

6. Winepress will be Trampled (Rev 14:19–20)

> [19]*So the angel thrust his sickle into the earth and gathered the vine of the earth, and threw it into the great winepress of the wrath of God.* [20]*And the winepress was trampled outside the city, and blood came out of the winepress, up to the horses' bridles, for one thousand six hundred furlongs.*

Christ is outside the city of Jerusalem, and the blood will come up to the horses' bridles of about four feet. A thousand and six hundred furlongs is about 185 miles, the distance from Dan to Beersheba, which is all Israel.

- Is 34:3: "Also their slain shall be thrown out; their stench shall rise from their corpses, and the mountains shall be melted with their blood."

7. God's Temple in Heaven will be Filled with Glory (Rev 15:1–8)

> [1]*Then I saw another sign in heaven, great and marvelous: seven angels having the seven last plagues, for in them the wrath of God is complete.* [2]*And I saw something like a sea of glass mingled with fire, and those who have the victory over the beast, over his image and over his mark and over the number of his name, standing on the sea of glass, having harps of God.* [3]*They sing the song of Moses, the servant of God, and the song of the Lamb, saying: "Great and marvelous are Your works, Lord God Almighty! Just and true are Your ways, O King of the saints!"*

The time is midpoint plus two and a half months, 1,335 days. John now sees a picture of heaven and the victorious saints celebrating the Lord's victory. In Revelation, the victory is always celebrated before the action takes place.

- Da 12:12: "Blessed is he who waits, and comes to the one thousand three hundred and thirty-five days."

> [4]*Who shall not fear You, O Lord, and glorify Your name? For You alone are holy. For all nations shall come and worship before You, For Your judgments have been manifested.* [5]*After these things I looked, and behold, the temple of the tabernacle of the testimony in heaven was opened.* [6]*And out of the temple came the seven angels having the seven plagues, clothed in pure bright linen, and having their chests girded with golden bands.* [7]*Then one of the four living creatures gave to the seven angels seven golden bowls full of the wrath of God who lives forever and ever.* [8]*The temple was filled with smoke from the glory of God and from His power, and no one was able to enter the temple till the seven plagues of the seven angels were completed.*

John sees the temple in heaven with seven angels dressed in priestly garments. The Shekinah glory in Exodus 40 and again in 1 Kings 8 was a cloud of smoke indicating the presence of God. This is the grace of God seen in His judgment. The angels are preparing for the Battle of Armageddon. Exodus 15 gave us a description of the celebration of Israel before the Passover when Israel was finally released from Egypt.

- Ex 15:1–21: "Then Moses and the children of Israel sang this song to the Lord, and spoke, saying: 'I will sing to the Lord for He has triumphed gloriously! The horse and its rider He has thrown into the sea! The Lord is my strength and song, and He has become my salvation; He is my God, and I will praise Him; my father's God, and I will exalt Him. The Lord is a man of war; the Lord is His name. Pharaoh's chariots and his army He has cast into the sea; His chosen captains also are drowned in the Red Sea. The depths have covered them; they sank to the bottom like a stone. Your right hand, O Lord, has become glorious in power; Your right hand, O Lord, has dashed the enemy in pieces. And in the greatness of Your excellence You have overthrown those who rose against You; You sent forth Your wrath; it consumed them like stubble. And with the blast of Your nostrils the waters were gathered together; the floods stood upright like a heap; and the depths congealed in the heart of the sea.' The enemy said, 'I will pursue, I will overtake, I will divide the spoil; my desire shall be satisfied on them. I will draw my sword, my hand shall destroy them.' You blew with Your wind, the sea covered them; they sank like lead in the mighty waters. Who is like You, O Lord, among the gods? Who is like You, glorious in holiness, fearful in praises, doing wonders? You stretched out Your right hand; the earth swallowed them. You in Your mercy have led forth the people whom You have redeemed; You have guided them in Your strength to Your holy habitation. The people will hear and be afraid; sorrow will take hold of the inhabitants of Palestine. Then the chiefs of Edom will be dismayed; the mighty men of Moab, trembling will take hold of them; all the inhabitants of Canaan will melt away. Fear and dread will fall on them; by the greatness of Your arm they will be as still as a stone, till Your people pass over, O Lord, till the people pass over whom You have purchased. You will bring them in and plant them in the mountain of Your inheritance, in the place, O Lord, which Your hands have made for Your own dwelling, the sanctuary O Lord which Your hands have established. The Lord shall reign forever and ever.' For the horses of Pharaoh went with his chariots and his horsemen into the sea, and the Lord brought back the waters of the sea upon them. But the children of Israel went on dry land in the midst of the sea. Then Miriam the prophetess, the sister of Aaron, l took the timbrel in her hand; and all the women went out after her with timbrels and with dances. And Miriam answered them: 'Sing to the Lord for He has triumphed gloriously! The horse and its rider He has thrown into the sea!'"

- Isa 66:23: "'And it shall come to pass that from one New Moon to another, and from one Sabbath to another, all flesh shall come to worship before Me,' says the LORD."

Just as the Lord protected His people in the Exodus, so shall He do so here. Just as the Lord drew His sword and His right hand destroyed them, so shall He do so here. Jesus is the Life and the Light of the World. The first three judgments regard blood. These plagues will be upon those who have not accepted the blood of Jesus in repentance.

The next three regard light: first, the scorching of the sun like the most excessive suffering Jesus suffered during his scourging. Then darkness like the last three hours on the cross, then water dries up as did Jesus when all water and blood flowed out to take away the keys of the kingdom in the first advent. Now this will be executed upon all who rejected the Messiah.

CHAPTER 8

Revelation 16: The Bowl Judgments

God is taking back everything He created for humanity because it became corrupt. God will deliver His wrath on those who wear the mark of the Beast. The prior seal and trumpet judgments were intended to convince all nations to repent and turn to the Lord. The bowl judgments are given upon Satan and all nations that came against God and His people. These are the final judgments and will complete the pouring out of the wrath of God on humanity. We will notice the word *all* described as to the destruction of the earth and those with the mark of the Beast. These judgments will be poured out in succession.

Seven Bowl Judgments

First Bowl	**All** will be afflicted with foul sores.
Second Bowl	**All** seas will be filled with blood; all sea creatures will die.
Third Bowl	**All** rivers will be filled with blood for killing martyrs.
Fourth Bowl	**All** those on the earth will be scorched by the sun.
Fifth Bowl	**All** darkness and great pain will overcome them.
Sixth Bowl	Euphrates River is **ALL** dried up for Battle of Armageddon to occur.
Seventh Bowl	Christ returns to earth for the second coming.

1. First Bowl (Rev 16:1–2)

> [1]*Then I heard a loud voice from the temple saying to the seven angels, "Go and pour out the bowls of the wrath of God on the earth."* [2]*So the first went and poured out his bowl upon the earth, and a foul and loathsome sore came upon the men who had the mark of the beast and those who worshiped his image.*

All those against God will be afflicted with foul-smelling, painful sores, and God will not allow them to die, nor will they heal. The sores people receive in the first plague will be present through all the bowl judgments. Then the drinking water is unavailable and continues throughout this time, while the earth and all those against God will be scorched by the sun. This continues until all is dark and perhaps the sun burns out. How do all the armies of the world come to the valley of Megiddo in this darkness, pained, and thirst-quenched state? There is much we cannot comprehend as we see the end of the earth as we know it today.

- Ex 9:9–11: "And it will become fine dust in all the land of Egypt, and it will cause boils that break out in sores on man and beast throughout all the land of Egypt. Then they took ashes from the furnace and stood before Pharaoh, and Moses scattered them toward heaven. And they caused boils that break out in sores on man and beast. And the magicians could not stand before Moses because of the boils, for the boils were on the magicians and on all the Egyptians."

2. Second Bowl (Rev 16:3)

> [3]*Then the second angel poured out his bowl on the sea, and it became blood as of a dead man; and every living creature in the sea died.*

The seas will all become filled with blood, and all the sea creatures will die. This same plague came upon the Egyptians in Exodus 7:14, when the Nile was turned into blood and all the fish died.

- Ex 7:17–21: "Thus says the Lord: 'By this you shall know that I am the Lord. Behold, I will strike the waters which are in the river with the rod that is in my hand, and they shall be turned to blood. And the fish that are in the river shall die, the river shall stink, the Egyptians will loathe to drink the water of the river.' Then the Lord spoke to Moses, 'Say to Aaron, 'Take your rod and stretch out your hand over the waters of Egypt, over their streams, over their rivers, over their ponds, and over all their pools of water, that they may become blood. And there shall be blood throughout all the land of Egypt, both in vessels of wood and vessels of stone.' And Moses and Aaron did so, just as the Lord commanded. So he lifted up the rod and struck and waters that were in the river, in the sight of Pharaoh and in the sight of his servants. And all the waters that were in the river were turned to blood. The fish that were in the river died, the river stank, and the Egyptians could not drink the water of the river. So there was blood throughout all the land of Egypt."

3. Third Bowl (Rev 16:4–7)

> *[4]Then the third angel poured out his bowl on the rivers and springs of water, and they became blood. [5]And I heard the angel of the waters saying: "You are righteous, O Lord, the One who is and who was and who is to be, because You have judged these things. [6]For they have shed the blood of saints and prophets, And You have given them blood to drink. For it is their just due." [7]And I heard another from the altar saying, "Even so, Lord God Almighty, true and righteous are Your judgments."*

Rivers will all become filled with the blood of those who killed martyrs. There will be no drinking water.

- Isa 49:26: "I will feed those who oppress you with their own flesh, and they shall be drunk with their own blood as with sweet wine. All flesh shall know that I, the LORD, *am* your Savior, and your Redeemer, the Mighty One of Jacob."

4. Fourth Bowl (Rev 16:8–9)

> *[8]Then the fourth angel poured out his bowl on the sun, and power was given to him to scorch men with fire. [9]And men were scorched with great heat, and they blasphemed the name of God who has power over these plagues; and they did not repent and give Him glory.*

The sun will scorch all the earth; the people too will be scorched and will all blaspheme God, but all will not repent.

- Mal 4:1: "For behold, the day is coming, burning like an oven, and all the proud, yes, all who do wickedly will be stubble. And the day which is coming shall burn them up," says the LORD of hosts, "That will leave them neither root nor branch."

5. Fifth Bowl (Rev 16:10–11)

> *[10] Then the fifth angel poured out his bowl on the throne of the beast, and his kingdom became full of darkness; and they gnawed their tongues because of the pain. [11]They blasphemed the God of heaven because of their pains and their sores, and did not repent of their deeds.*

Darkness and great pain will come to all; however, they will continue to blaspheme instead of repent. There will be no sun in the new earth in chapter 21. Is it possible that the sun has ceased to exist here? What we see is everything that God gave humanity He is taking away. If we go back to Genesis 1, God is taking back everything He created that became corrupted by Satan.

6. Sixth Bowl (Rev 16:12–16)

> *[12] Then the sixth angel poured out his bowl on the great river Euphrates, and its water was dried up, so that the way of the kings from the east [Far East is China and India] might be prepared.*

The Euphrates River will all be dried up, and all wicked nations, including the spirit demons, will converge on Israel for supremacy in the Battle of Armageddon, where the Antichrist will be destroyed. Nothing has changed of the last five plagues that the Lord placed on humanity.

> *[13]And I saw three unclean spirits like frogs coming out of the mouth of the dragon, out of the mouth of the beast, and out of the mouth of the false prophet. [14]For they are spirits of demons, performing signs, which go out to the kings of the earth and of the whole world, to gather them to the battle of that great day of God Almighty. [15]"Behold, I am coming as a thief. Blessed is he who watches, and keeps his garments, lest he walk naked and they see his shame." [16]And they gathered them together to the place called in Hebrew, Armageddon.*

This is the only time Scripture mentions the word *Armageddon*. John is telling us about the Battle of Armageddon that will not happen until chapter 19. In our timeline, we see that the earth is dark, so therefore, the army is being formed to come as a thief. The Antichrist is preparing the whole world to come against God.

- Zec 12:10–11: "And I will pour on the house of David and on the inhabitants of Jerusalem the Spirit of grace and supplication; then they will look on Me whom they pierced. Yes, they will mourn for Him as one mourns for his only son, and grieve for Him as one grieves for a firstborn. In that day there shall be a great mourning in Jerusalem, like the mourning at Hadad Rimmon in the plain of Megiddo."

7. Seventh Bowl (Rev 16:17–21)

> *[17]Then the seventh angel poured out his bowl into the air, and a loud voice came out of the temple of heaven, from the throne, saying, "It is done!" [18]And there were noises and thunderings and lightnings; and there was a great earthquake, such a mighty and great earthquake as had not occurred since men*

> *were on the earth. [19]Now the great city was divided into three parts, and the cities of the nations fell. And great Babylon was remembered before God, to give her the cup of the wine of the fierceness of His wrath. [20]Then every island fled away, and the mountains were not found. [21]And great hail from heaven fell upon men, each hailstone about the weight of a talent. Men blasphemed God because of the plague of the hail, since that plague was exceedingly great.*

God pronounces, "It is done!" This is different from God resting in Genesis 2 after His work or Jesus saying, "It is finished" at the cross after His work. Now, God is saying, "It is over and done with." The wrath of God planned from the beginning of time for those who did not worship Him has been poured out. It is done! His Word has been spoken, and now it will happen.

These verses are prophesying that Christ will return to earth for the second coming in Revelation 19. Christ's feet will touch ground at the Mount of Olives (Ac 1:9–12); this event will trigger the great, earth-changing earthquake described in Zechariah 14:4–5. God will destroy Babylon with thunder, lightning, an earthquake, and hundred-pound hail, the likes of which we have never seen before. Jerusalem will be split by the earthquake. It is done!

- Zec 14:4–5: "And in that day His feet will stand on the Mount of Olives, which faces Jerusalem on the east. And the Mount of Olives shall be split in two, from east to west, making a very large valley; half of the mountain shall move toward the north and half of it toward the south. Then you shall flee through My mountain valley, for the mountain valley shall reach to Azal. Yes, you shall flee as you fled from the earthquake In the days of Uzziah king of Judah. Thus the LORD my God will come, And all the saints with You."

CHAPTER 9

Revelation 17–19: Christ's Victory over Babylon

Chapters 14 and 15 gave us an overview of the climax leading to the Battle of Armageddon. Chapter 16 gave us a description of the seven vial judgments that will come just before Christ returns to the earth to gain victory over the Antichrist so He can place Satan in the bottomless pit for a thousand years while Christ rules on earth in chapter 19. Chapter 17 shows the fall of Babylon, and the Antichrist is overcome in chapter 18 at Armageddon. Here is an overview of chapters 17–19.

1. One-World Religious System is Destroyed (Rev 17:1–18)
2. One-World Government and Financial Systems are Destroyed (Rev 18:1–20)
3. Babylon's Fall (Rev 18:21–24)
4. Heaven Exalts over Babylon (Rev 19:1–7)
5. Marriage Supper of the Lamb (Rev 19:8–10)
6. Christ Comes to Armageddon (Rev 19:11–20)
7. Antichrist and Antispirit are Cast into the Lake of Fire (Rev 19:20–21)

This overview of chapters shows that the same scenario is happening repeatedly, giving more details of the same timeline.

Chap 14-15 (Proclamations) . Hour has come
. Babylon will Fall
. 666; Wrath
. Bowl judgments will be poured out
. Climax in Battle of Armageddon
. Fire will destroy Satan
. Blood will rise to horses' bridles

Chap 16 (Bowl Judgments) . All inflicted with foul sores
. All seas filled w/blood; All sea creatures die
. All rivers will be filled with blood
. All scorched by the sun
. All darkness & great pain
. Euphrates will dry up for Battle
. Christ returns for Second Coming

Chap 17-19 (Christ's victory). One World Religion
. One World Govt & Financial System
. Babylon's Fall
. Heaven Exults Over Babylon
. Marriage Supper of the Lamb
. Christ comes to Armageddon
. Antichrist & Antispirit cast into Lake of Fire

1. One-World Religious System Is Destroyed (Rev 17:1–18)

> *[1]Then one of the seven angels who had the seven bowls came and talked with me, saying to me, "Come, I will show you the judgment of the great harlot who sits on many waters, [2]with whom the kings of the earth committed fornication, and the inhabitants of the earth were made drunk with the wine of her fornication."*

The great harlot is also called Babylon and represents the revised Roman Empire. The harlot sitting on many waters indicates all the people of every nation. Babylon symbolizes the satanic worldly system and all who have come against God forever. This judgment is described in chapter 18.

- Jer 51:7–13: "Babylon was a golden cup in the LORD's hand that made all the earth drunk. The nations drank her wine; therefore the nations are deranged. Babylon has suddenly fallen and been destroyed. Wail for her! Take balm for her pain; perhaps she may be healed. We would have healed Babylon, but she is not healed. Forsake her, and let us go everyone to his own country; for her judgment reaches to heaven and is lifted up to the skies. The LORD has revealed our righteousness. Come and let us declare in Zion the work of the LORD our God. Make the arrows bright! Gather the shields! The LORD has raised up the spirit of the kings of the Medes. For His plan is against Babylon to destroy it, because it is the vengeance of the LORD, the vengeance for His temple. Set up the standard on the walls of Babylon; make the guard strong, set up the watchmen, prepare the ambushes. For the LORD has both devised and done what He spoke against the inhabitants of Babylon. O you who dwell by many waters, abundant in treasures, your end has come, the measure of your covetousness."
- Na 3:4: "Because of the multitude of harlotries of the seductive harlot, the mistress of sorceries, who sells nations through her harlotries, and families through her sorceries."

> [3]*So he carried me away in the Spirit into the wilderness. And I saw a woman sitting on a scarlet beast which was full of names of blasphemy, having seven heads and ten horns.*

The woman, organized religion, was in the wilderness, no doubt looking for Israel.

> [4]*The woman was arrayed in purple and scarlet, and adorned with gold and precious stones and pearls, having in her hand a golden cup full of abominations and the filthiness of her fornication.*

This woman, the great prostitute, signifies all wealth, materialism, and immorality. Purple was the color worn by the Roman emperor and his statesman. The golden cup full of abominations is the religious system of Antichrist.

> [5]*And on her forehead a name was written: MYSTERY, BABYLON THE GREAT, THE MOTHER OF HARLOTS AND OF THE ABOMINATIONS OF THE EARTH.* [6]*I saw the woman, drunk with the blood of the saints and with the blood of the martyrs of Jesus. And when I saw her, I marveled with great amazement.*

The mystery is now being revealed. Babylon is actually the mother of all iniquity. She was drunk with the blood of the saints, and that was her purpose in everything evil she did.

- 2Th 2:7: "For the mystery of lawlessness is already at work; only He who now restrains will do so until He is taken out of the way."

> [7]*But the angel said to me, "Why did you marvel? I will tell you the mystery of the woman and of the beast that carries her, which has the seven heads and the ten horns.* [8]*The beast that you saw was, and is not, and will ascend out of the bottomless pit and go to perdition. And those who dwell on the earth will marvel, whose names are not written in the Book of Life from the foundation of the world, when they see the beast that was, and is not, and yet is.* [9]*Here is the mind which has wisdom: The seven heads are seven mountains on which the woman sits.* [10]*There are also seven kings. Five have fallen, one is, and the other has not yet come. And when he comes, he must continue a short time.* [11]*The beast that was, and is not, is himself also the eighth, and is of the seven, and is going to perdition.* [12]*The ten horns which you saw are ten kings who have received no kingdom as yet, but they receive authority for one hour as kings with the beast.* [13]*These are of one mind, and they will give their power and authority to the beast.* [14]*These will make war with the Lamb, and the Lamb will overcome them, for He is Lord of lords and King of kings; and those who are with Him are called, chosen, and faithful."* [15]*Then*

he said to me, "The waters which you saw, where the harlot sits, are peoples, multitudes, nations, and tongues. [16]And the ten horns which you saw on the beast, these will hate the harlot, make her desolate and naked, eat her flesh and burn her with fire. [17]For God has put it into their hearts to fulfill His purpose, to be of one mind, and to give their kingdom to the beast, until the words of God are fulfilled. [18]And the woman whom you saw is that great city which reigns over the kings of the earth."

John explains the mystery: the seven heads or kings under the Beast control the religious system. Five empires were destroyed, one exists, and one hasn't come yet. Then we see ten horns, the kings or leaders of the nations in the European Union, which is the revived Roman Empire. They will rule the world government and financial systems.

- Ez 16:37–38: "Surely, therefore, I will gather all your lovers with whom you took pleasure, all those you loved, and all those you hated; I will gather them from all around against you and will uncover your nakedness to them, that they may see all your nakedness. And I will judge you as women who break wedlock or shed blood are judged; I will bring blood upon you in fury and jealousy."
- Da 7:20: "And the ten horns that were on its head, and the other horn which came up, before which three fell, namely, that horn which had eyes and a mouth which spoke pompous words, whose appearance was greater than his fellows."
- 1Ti 6:15: "… which He will manifest in His own time, He who is the blessed and only Potentate, the King of kings and Lord of lords."
- 1Th 2:11: "… as you know how we exhorted, and comforted, and charged every one of you, as a father does his own children."

What is the difference between the UN, NATO, and the EU (2015)?

- The UN (United Nations) was established in 1945 as an international body to solve world political disputes. As a result of this organization, the League of Nations ended in 1948. The UN's role is to enforce international law for all countries around the world. The UN includes 193 member nations and is headquartered in New York City.

- NATO (North Atlantic Treaty Organization) is an international military organization made up of twenty-eight nations across North America and Europe.
- The EU (European Union) comprises twenty-eight members primarily focused on Europe leading the world. Ten nations are full members of the EU today under the Western European Alliance. This could be those ten nations we discussed as the revised Roman Empire. These ten nations are also members of NATO: Belgium, France, Germany, Greece, Italy, Luxembourg, Netherlands, Portugal, Spain, and United Kingdom. The EU is making a case to create its own army and to make the euro a one-world currency.

2. One-World Government and Financial Systems are Destroyed (Rev 18:1–20)

> [1]*After these things I saw another angel coming down from heaven, having great authority, and the earth was illuminated with his glory.* [2a]*And he cried mightily with a loud voice, saying, "Babylon the great is fallen, is fallen."*

Notice that this angel illuminated the dark earth with the glory of God.

- Isa 14:23: "'I will also make it a possession for the porcupine, and marshes of muddy water; I will sweep it with the broom of destruction,' says the LORD of hosts."
- Ez 43:2: "And behold, the glory of the God of Israel came from the way of the east. His voice was like the sound of many waters; and the earth shone with His glory."

> [2b]*and has become a dwelling place of demons, a prison for every foul spirit, and a cage for every unclean and hated bird!*

Babylon has always been the headquarters of Satan.

- Isa 13:19: "And Babylon, the glory of kingdoms, the beauty of the Chaldeans' pride, will be as when God overthrew Sodom and Gomorrah."

> [3]*For all the nations have drunk of the wine of the wrath of her fornication, the kings of the earth have committed fornication with her, and the merchants of the earth have become rich through the abundance of her luxury."* [4]*And I heard another voice from heaven saying, "Come out of her, my people, lest you share in her sins, and lest you receive of her plagues.* [5]*For her sins have reached to heaven, and God has remembered her iniquities.* [6]*Render to her just as she rendered to you, and repay her double according to her works; in the cup which she has mixed, mix double for her.* [7]*In the measure that she glorified herself and lived luxuriously, in the same measure give her torment and sorrow; for she says in her heart, 'I sit as queen, and am no widow, and will not see sorrow.'* [8]*Therefore her plagues will come in one day—death and mourning and famine. And she will be utterly burned with fire, for strong is the Lord God who judges her.*

The voice of probably Jesus is crying out, "Come out of her, my people, lest you share in her sins, and lest you receive of her plagues." These will be the last plagues of judgment before the final victory. Notice once more that there are people on earth who will live through the millennium.

- Isa 47:15: "Thus shall they be to you with whom you have labored, your merchants from your youth; they shall wander each one to his quarter. No one shall save you."
- Isa 48:20: "Go forth from Babylon! Flee from the Chaldeans! With a voice of singing, declare, proclaim this, utter it to the end of the earth; say, 'The LORD has redeemed His servant Jacob!'"

> [9]*"The kings of the earth who committed fornication and lived luxuriously with her will weep and lament for her, when they*

see the smoke of her burning, [10]standing at a distance for fear of
her torment, saying, 'Alas, alas, that great city Babylon, that
mighty city! For in one hour your judgment has come.' [11]And
the merchants of the earth will weep and mourn over her, for
no one buys their merchandise anymore: [12]merchandise of gold
and silver, precious stones and pearls, fine linen and purple,
silk and scarlet, every kind of citron wood, every kind of object
of ivory, every kind of object of most precious wood, bronze,
iron, and marble; [13]and cinnamon and incense, fragrant oil
and frankincense, wine and oil, fine flour and wheat, cattle
and sheep, horses and chariots, and bodies and souls of men.
[14]The fruit that your soul longed for has gone from you, and
all the things which are rich and splendid have gone from you,
and you shall find them no more at all. [15]The merchants of these
things, who became rich by her, will stand at a distance for
fear of her torment, weeping and wailing, [16]and saying, 'Alas,
alas, that great city that was clothed in fine linen, purple, and
scarlet, and adorned with gold and precious stones and pearls!
[17]For in one hour such great riches came to nothing.' Every
shipmaster, all who travel by ship, sailors, and as many as
trade on the sea, stood at a distance [18]and cried out when they
saw the smoke of her burning, saying, 'What is like this great
city?' [19]They threw dust on their heads and cried out, weeping
and wailing, and saying, 'Alas, alas, that great city, in which
all who had ships on the sea became rich by her wealth! For in
one hour she is made desolate.' [20]Rejoice over her, O heaven,
and you holy apostles and prophets, for God has avenged you
on her!"

The Antichrist and the False Prophet will have left Babylon for Jerusalem to prepare for battle. They will see on TV Babylon destroyed just as Sodom and Gomorrah were. To bewail is to sob uncontrollably, and to lament is to be in anguish over the falling of the world systems. All the world's leaders will know this is done by the hand of God and their demise is coming quickly. Babylon is no more.

- Josh 7:6: "Then Joshua tore his clothes, and fell to the earth on his face before the ark of the LORD until evening, he and the elders of Israel; and they put dust on their heads."
- Isa 21:9: "'And look, here comes a chariot of men with a pair of horsemen!' Then he answered and said, 'Babylon is fallen, is fallen! And all the carved images of her gods He has broken to the ground.'"
- Isa 23:14: "Wail, you ships of Tarshish! For your strength is laid waste."
- Jer 51:48: "'Then the heavens and the earth and all that is in them shall sing joyously over Babylon; for the plunderers shall come to her from the north,' says the LORD."
- Ez 27:13–34: "Javan, Tubal, and Meshech were your traders. They bartered human lives and vessels of bronze for your merchandise. Those from the house of Togarmah traded for your wares with horses, steeds, and mules. The men of Dedan were your traders; many isles were the market of your hand. They brought you ivory tusks and ebony as payment. Syria was your merchant because of the abundance of goods you made. They gave you for your wares emeralds, purple, embroidery, fine linen, corals, and rubies. Judah and the land of Israel were your traders. They traded for your merchandise wheat of Minnith, millet, honey, oil, and balm. Damascus was your merchant because of the abundance of goods you made, because of your many luxury items, with the wine of Helbon and with white wool. Dan and Javan paid for your wares, traversing back and forth. Wrought iron, cassia, and cane were among your merchandise. Dedan was your merchant in saddlecloths for riding. Arabia and all the princes of Kedar were your regular merchants. They traded with you in lambs, rams, and goats. The merchants of Sheba and Raamah were your merchants. They traded for your wares the choicest spices, all kinds of precious stones, and gold. Haran, Canneh, Eden, the merchants of Sheba, Assyria, and Chilmad were your merchants. These were your merchants in choice items—in purple clothes, in embroidered garments, in chests of multicolored apparel, in sturdy woven cords, which were in your marketplace. The ships

of Tarshish were carriers of your merchandise. You were filled and very glorious in the midst of the seas. Your oarsmen brought you into many waters, but the east wind broke you in the midst of the seas. Your riches, wares, and merchandise, your mariners and pilots, your caulkers and merchandisers, all your men of war who are in you, and the entire company which is in your midst, will fall into the midst of the seas on the day of your ruin. The common-land will shake at the sound of the cry of your pilots. All who handle the oar, the mariners, all the pilots of the sea will come down from their ships and stand on the shore. They will make their voice heard because of you; they will cry bitterly and cast dust on their heads; they will roll about in ashes; they will shave themselves completely bald because of you, gird themselves with sackcloth, and weep for you with bitterness of heart and bitter wailing. In their wailing for you they will take up a lamentation, and lament for you: 'What city is like Tyre, destroyed in the midst of the sea? When your wares went out by sea, you satisfied many people; you enriched the kings of the earth with your many luxury goods and your merchandise. But you are broken by the seas in the depths of the waters; your merchandise and the entire company will fall in your midst.'"

- Lk 11:49: "Therefore the wisdom of God also said, 'I will send them prophets and apostles, and some of them they will kill and persecute.'"

3. Babylon's Fall (Rev 18:21–24)

> *[21]Then a mighty angel took up a stone like a great millstone and threw it into the sea, saying, "Thus with violence the great city Babylon shall be thrown down, and shall not be found anymore. [22]The sound of harpists, musicians, flutists, and trumpeters shall not be heard in you anymore. No craftsman of any craft shall be found in you anymore, and the sound of a millstone shall not be heard in you anymore. [23]The light of a lamp shall not shine in you anymore, and the voice of bridegroom and bride shall not be heard in you anymore. For*

> *your merchants were the great men of the earth, for by your sorcery all the nations were deceived.* [24]*And in her was found the blood of prophets and saints, and of all who were slain on the earth."*

Babylon is gone, but not the Antichrist. Finally, Jesus returns to earth with His army of Christians, as they are now His priests and kings. Finally, the day of the Lord has come. Jesus will defeat the Antichrist on this one day.

- 2Ki 9:22: "Now it happened, when Joram saw Jehu, that he said, 'Is it peace, Jehu?' So he answered, 'What peace, as long as the harlotries of your mother Jezebel and her witchcraft are so many?'"
- Jer 7:34: "Then I will cause to cease from the cities of Judah and from the streets of Jerusalem the voice of mirth and the voice of gladness, the voice of the bridegroom and the voice of the bride. For the land shall be desolate."
- Jer 16:9: "For thus says the LORD of hosts, the God of Israel: 'Behold, I will cause to cease from this place, before your eyes and in your days, the voice of mirth and the voice of gladness, the voice of the bridegroom and the voice of the bride.'"
- Jer 25:10: "Moreover I will take from them the voice of mirth and the voice of gladness, the voice of the bridegroom and the voice of the bride, the sound of the millstones and the light of the lamp."
- Jer 51:60–64: "So Jeremiah wrote in a book all the evil that would come upon Babylon, all these words that are written against Babylon. And Jeremiah said to Seraiah, 'When you arrive in Babylon and see it, and read all these words, then you shall say, "O LORD, You have spoken against this place to cut it off, so that none shall remain in it, neither man nor beast, but it shall be desolate forever." Now it shall be, when you have finished reading this book, that you shall tie a stone to it and throw it out into the Euphrates. Then you shall say, "Thus Babylon shall sink and not rise from the catastrophe that I will bring upon her. And they shall be weary."'"

4. Heaven Exults over Babylon (Rev 19:1–7)

> [1]*After these things I heard a loud voice of a great multitude in heaven, saying, "Alleluia! Salvation and glory and honor and power belong to the Lord our God!* [2]*For true and righteous are His judgments, because He has judged the great harlot who corrupted the earth with her fornication; and He has avenged on her the blood of His servants shed by her."* [3]*Again they said, "Alleluia! Her smoke rises up forever and ever!"* [4]*And the twenty-four elders and the four living creatures fell down and worshiped God who sat on the throne, saying, "Amen! Alleluia!"* [5]*Then a voice came from the throne, saying, "Praise our God, all you His servants and those who fear Him, both small and great!"* [6]*And I heard, as it were, the voice of a great multitude, as the sound of many waters and as the sound of mighty thunderings, saying, "Alleluia! For the Lord God Omnipotent reigns!* [7]*Let us be glad and rejoice and give Him glory, for the marriage of the Lamb has come, and His wife has made herself ready."*

Now we see the word *hallelujah* four times. Hallelujah means to praise Yahweh. God's people are praising Yahweh, God Almighty, because Babylon is no more. We can recite Psalm 113 aloud to praise the Lord.

- Psalm 113:
  "Praise the LORD!
  Praise, O servants of the LORD,
  Praise the name of the LORD!
  Blessed be the name of the LORD
  From this time forth and forevermore!
  From the rising of the sun to its going down
  The LORD's name is to be praised.
  The LORD is high above all nations,
  His glory above the heavens.
  Who is like the LORD our God,
  Who dwells on high,

Who humbles Himself to behold
The things that are in the heavens and in the earth?
He raises the poor out of the dust,
And lifts the needy out of the ash heap,
That He may seat him with princes—
With the princes of His people.
He grants the barren woman a home,
Like a joyful mother of children.
Praise the LORD!"

5. Marriage Supper of the Lamb (Rev 19:8–10)

> *8And to her it was granted to be arrayed in fine linen, clean and bright, for the fine linen is the righteous acts of the saints. 9Then he said to me, "Write: 'Blessed are those who are called to the marriage supper of the Lamb!'" And he said to me, "These are the true sayings of God." 10And I fell at his feet to worship him. But he said to me, "See that you do not do that! I am your fellow servant, and of your brethren who have the testimony of Jesus. Worship God! For the testimony of Jesus is the spirit of prophecy."*

The testimony of Jesus is the spirit of prophecy. Because of the finished work on the cross, every prophecy in the Old and New Testaments regarding the Lord as our Messiah has come true. All heaven, the Jews, Gentiles, Christians, and the heavenly host are worshiping the Messiah, the Lord Jesus Christ. He is the King of the universe and is everlasting.

- 1Ch 16:36: "Blessed be the LORD God of Israel from everlasting to everlasting! And all the people said, 'Amen!' and praised the LORD."
- Ps 134:1: "Behold, bless the LORD, all you servants of the LORD, who by night stand in the house of the LORD!"
- Isa 34:8-10: "For it is the day of the LORD's vengeance, the year of recompense for the cause of Zion. Its streams shall be turned into pitch, and its dust into brimstone; its land shall become burning

pitch. It shall not be quenched night or day; its smoke shall ascend forever. From generation to generation it shall lie waste; no one shall pass through it forever and ever."

- Ez 1:24: "When they went, I heard the noise of their wings, like the noise of many waters, like the voice of the Almighty, a tumult like the noise of an army; and when they stood still, they let down their wings."
- Ro 7:4: "Therefore, my brethren, you also have become dead to the law through the body of Christ, that you may be married to another—to Him who was raised from the dead, that we should bear fruit to God."
- 2Co 11:2: " For I am jealous for you with godly jealousy. For I have betrothed you to one husband, that I may present you as a chaste virgin to Christ."
- Heb 1:14: "Are they not all ministering spirits sent forth to minister for those who will inherit salvation?"
- 1Jn 5:10: "He who believes in the Son of God has the witness in himself; he who does not believe God has made Him a liar, because he has not believed the testimony that God has given of His Son."

We are finally celebrating the marriage of the Lamb. Notice that it doesn't say bride but Lamb. This is the coronation of King Jesus to the promised bride, the church. The bride is called New Jerusalem in chapter 21:2–10. According to Romans 7:4, 2 Corinthians 11:2, and Ephesians 5:23–32, the church is the chaste virgin bride of Christ. The wedding banquet is described in Matthew 22:1–14 in a parable about a king who invites his servants to the wedding of his son. When they (Israel) do not accept the invitation, an invitation was sent to more servants. This parable shows that Israel is not the church, the bride of Christ, because Israel rejected Christ. It was the church that accepted the invitation of Christ. Others who accepted the invitation here in Revelation are all those saints who came to Christ throughout the tribulation. They will be guests at the wedding.

The ancient Jewish wedding has four stages.

1. Formal Contract: According to ancient Jewish wedding customs, *ketubbah* was a legal document signed by two witnesses betrothing the man and woman and was considered the marriage covenant. A glass of wine was set before the bride, and if she accepted it, that meant she accepted the proposal.

   When Christians come to Christ, the Holy Spirit accepts them legally as one written in the Lamb's Book of Life. The Holy Spirit comes to dwell in the believers and cleanses them in preparation for their marriage to King Jesus. Christ paid the price for His bride (1Co 6:20; Eph 5:25). Christ went to heaven to prepare a place for His bride (Jn 14:1–3).

   According to ancient Jewish custom, the bridegroom adds a room on to his father's house. When the father deems the room ready, he sends out an announcement to the guests. When Christians declare themselves to Christ, they are betrothed or engaged. The Holy Spirit comes to dwell, chaperone, and cleanse them in preparation for the bridegroom.

2. Claiming the bride: According to ancient Jewish wedding customs, the bridegroom comes as a thief in the night, so she must be always ready. This is the rapture, when Jesus takes His bride to His Father's house (1Th 4:13–18).

3. Wedding Feast: The marriage ceremony is held under a *chupah* (canopy). The ketubbah is read, and the ring is placed on the bride's finger. Then seven blessings are said over the couple followed by another glass of wine. This glass is broken by the groom, which is symbolic of the destruction of Jerusalem. The couple goes to the room the bridegroom has prepared and stays there for seven days (time of tribulation is seven years). The father arranges for provisions. The family and friends gather during the week and feast in celebration. At the end of the seven days, the couple joins the guests and rejoices with them at the marriage supper.

4. Living together: The bridegroom does not work for a year; he spends that time with the bride to create a relationship. The

millennium will not be one year but one thousand years, and there will be no divorce. The bridegroom, the King of the kingdom of God, will rule over the kingdom with His bride forever.

6. Christ Comes to Armageddon (Rev 19:11–20a)

Scenario of the Battle of Armageddon

Tribulation Timeline

.--.

. Antichrist sets up his HQ in Rome while Temple is built in Jerusalem and city of Babylon built.
. Peace treaty is confirmed.
. Everyone believes Antichrist is the Messiah who returned to set up his kingdom.
. During first-half, Antichrist wars in order to establish his kingdom.
. He overthrows three kings, then the rest of the ten surrender (Dan 7:23) by Mid-Trib.

  . At Mid Trib Antichrist – abomination of desolation – declares He is God in the Temple. Requires mark (666) and all to worship him as god.

    . During last 3 ½ years (Great Trib) HQ in Babylon.
    . Leaves Babylon for Jerusalem to wipe out Jews.
    . Once leaves, God destroys city of Babylon.
    . Antichrist fights to take over Jews in Jerusalem.
    . Slaughters 5/6 of the Jews (Ez 39:2).
    . Christ returns, steps on Mt Olives, splits east/west.
    . Antichrist flees to Megiddo with armies of world.
    . Jews protected, Christ slays w/sword of mouth.
    . Daniel 12:12 – rebuild Jerusalem.
    . Jesus enters Eastern Gate w/saints, reigns.

This scenario is covered in three different Old Testament Scriptures.

- ❖ Daniel 11:36-45 shows the events of Antichrist to prepare for the battle.
- ❖ Ezekiel 38 shows the nations that will come against Israel.
- ❖ Zechariah 14 shows the events of the Lord when He comes back to win the battle.

❖ <u>Daniel 11:36-45 shows the events of Antichrist to prepare for the battle.</u>

- Dan 11:36: "Then the king shall do according to his own will: he shall exalt and magnify himself above every god, shall speak blasphemies against the God of gods, and shall prosper till the wrath has been accomplished; for what has been determined shall be done. He shall regard neither the God of his fathers nor the desire of women, nor regard any god; for he shall exalt himself above them all. But in their place he shall honor a god of fortresses; and a god which his fathers did not know he shall honor with gold and silver, with precious stones and pleasant things. Thus he shall act against the strongest fortresses with a foreign god, which he shall acknowledge, and advance its glory; and he shall cause them to rule over many, and divide the land for gain."

At the beginning of the tribulation, the king (the Antichrist) magnified himself above every god. We must realize that the Antichrist came as the Messiah to the Jews and as the Mahdi to the Islamic faith. All religions are waiting for the Messiah to come. The Antichrist will regard himself above all religions of the world. All worship is to him. Satan originally wanted to be worshiped as God, which is the reason he was sent from heaven according to Isaiah 14 and Ezekiel 28. Even when he approached Jesus to test Him in Luke 4, it was all about Satan wanting to be worshiped. Antichrist breaks the peace treaty and this begins his demise.

- Da 11:40a: "At the time of the end the king of the South shall attack him."

The Antichrist began his reign with headquarters in Rome while the temple is being built in Jerusalem and while Babylon is being restored to its original beauty as one of the seven wonders of the ancient world. His army would be under the authority of the European Union, of which he is the little horn, the leader.

Israel is a small country stretching nearly 260 miles from north to south, and approximately 70 miles at the widest point. It borders Lebanon to the north and Syria to the northeast; it has about a 150-mile border with Jordan to the east, a gulf port on the Red Sea, Egypt to the southwest, and the Mediterranean Sea to the west. It is very vulnerable for attack from any direction. Because it takes only minutes for any country to attack it, we can see why Israel had to build the iron dome defense shield in order to protect itself. Israel and all Christian nations are considered infidels to the Muslim-controlled countries that want to wipe them off of the face of the earth.

Four main power blocks will emerge led by four kings from the south, north, east, and west. Zechariah 14:2 says, "For I will gather all the nations to battle against Jerusalem."

The King of the South—Arab League

The Arab League has twenty-two member states: Algeria, Bahrain, Comoros, Djibouti, Egypt, Iraq, Jordan, Kuwait, Lebanon, Libya, Mauritania, Morocco, Oman, State of Palestine, Qatar, Saudi Arabia, Somalia, Sudan, Syria, Tunisia, United Arab Emirates, and Yemen. Notice that Iran is not a part of the Arab League.

- Da 11:40b: "And the king of the North shall come against him like a whirlwind, with chariots, horsemen, and with many ships; and he shall enter the countries, overwhelm them, and pass through."

The King of the North—Turkey or Russia

Turkey is 99 percent Islamic. Tayyip Erdogan is the prime minister of Turkey and wants to lead a coalition of nations in the Islamic war. What we actually see in the Middle East today is Shiite fighting Sunni to form one religion under Sharia law. We also see Putin not only supplying nuclear capacity to Iran but also looking to take control of countries to the west such as Ukraine to gain access to the Black Sea and regain the territory of the Communist bloc.

- Da 41a: "He shall also enter the Glorious Land, and many countries shall be overthrown."

At mid-tribulation, the Antichrist comes to the temple in New Jerusalem (the Glorious Land) and the abomination of desecration takes place (2Th 2:4). He requires everyone to worship him. He does away with Jewish sacrifices and sets up an image of himself (Rev 13:15).

- Da 41b-43: "But these shall escape from his hand: Edom, Moab, and the prominent people of Ammon. He shall stretch out his hand against the countries, and the land of Egypt shall not escape. He shall have power over the treasures of gold and silver, and over all the precious things of Egypt; also the Libyans and Ethiopians shall follow at his heels."

It seems that after Antichrist takes the throne in Jerusalem, the world knows he isn't their Messiah, and they come against him. Daniel 11:40 says that the king of the south over the Arab League pushes at him, and then the king of the north, Turkey, comes against him. It says he shall enter the countries and shall overflow and pass over—it looks like the Antichrist beats them.

Verse 41 says many countries shall be overthrown. This could be his domination over the Islamic states that were in arms over his taking over the Dome, their religious site in Jerusalem. Verse 41 says that Edom, Moab, and Ammon, that is, Jordan, escape his hand. This must be because the Jews were being protected in Petra, Jordan. Verse 42 says that he wars over Egypt, Libya, and Ethiopia—this must be the Arab League.

- Da 11:44-45: "But news from the east and the north shall trouble him; therefore he shall go out with great fury to destroy and annihilate many. And he shall plant the tents of his palace

> between the seas and the glorious holy mountain; yet he shall come to his end, and no one will help him."

At that point, verse 44 says an army from the east and north come against him, and this troubles him. Daniel 11 ends by saying he shall come to his end and none shall help him. This must be the arrival of Christ, which leads to the Battle of Armageddon.

The King of the East—Asia

The king of the east is the leader of the Asiatic powers lying to the east of the Euphrates. This power bloc may consist of modern Afghanistan, India, Pakistan, China, Japan, and Korea. When the eastern coalition marches on Israel, we are set up for the Battle of Armageddon.

The King of the West—New World Order

The Antichrist will be the leader of the revised Roman Empire. Could this be the European Union leading the new world order?

❖ Ezekiel 38 shows the nations that will come against Israel.

There are two battles described in Revelation. The Battle of Armageddon happens before the thousand-year rule of Christ, and the Battle of Gog and Magog happens after the millennium. The reference for these battles is in Ezekiel 38. However, Ezekiel 38 cross references Revelation 20, the war of Gog and Magog, not the Battle of Armageddon covered here in chapters 18 and 19.

In Ezekiel, all the nations come against Israel for the Battle of Armageddon. Therefore, a conclusion has to be drawn. Gog has to represent the Antichrist, who has been and always will be the adversary of God for all time until he is thrown into the lake of fire. Gog is the adversary in both battles.

- Ez 38: 1-6, 13: "Now the word of the Lord came to me, saying, 'Son of man, set your face against Gog, of the land of Magog,

> the prince of Rosh, Meshech, and Tubal, and prophesy against him, and say, "Thus says the Lord God: Behold, I *am* against you, O Gog, the prince of Rosh, Meshech, and Tubal. I will turn you around, put hooks into your jaws, and lead you out, with all your army, horses, and horsemen, all splendidly clothed, a great company with bucklers and shields, all of them handling swords. Persia, Ethiopia, and Libya are with them, all of them with shield and helmet; Gomer and all its troops; the house of Togarmah from the far north and all its troops—many people are with you."'" Verse 13, "Sheba, Dedan, the merchants of Tarshish, and all their young lions will say to you, 'Have you come to take plunder? Have you gathered your army to take booty, to carry away silver and gold, to take away livestock and goods, to take great plunder?'"

All the generations of Noah described in Genesis 10 will come together for the battle as depicted in Ezekiel 38 and 39. Here are the generations of Japheth (Gentiles) and Ham (Arabians) coming against Shem (Israel).

First we see the generations of Japheth, the Gentiles (Ge 10:2–5). The sons of Japheth were Gomer, Magog, Madai, Javan, Tubal, Meshech, and Tiras.

- **Gog** is from the land of Magog and rules over Rosh, Meshech, and Tubal (Ez 38:2). Gog is a person, not a place. Gog is the leader of the invasion against Israel and is from Magog. Gog and Magog are north of the Caspian and Black Seas. This supports the theory that the Antichrist is said to come from Russia.
- **Magog** is the second son of Japheth who located north of the Caspian and Black Seas. Josephus says that Magogians are Greeks and called Scythians. Scythians were nomads who inhabited Central Asia across the southern part of Russia. Today, the former Soviet republics of Kazakhstan, Kyrgyzstan, Uzbekistan, Turkmenistan, Tajikistan, and Northern Afghanistan are all of Islamic faith with a combined population of 60 million. According to Islamic teaching, Allah has decreed that Gog and Magog will pour out an attack on Israel from all directions.

- **Rosh** means to submit. The great Russian bear from the north will invade Israel.
- **Meshech** and **Tubal** were the sixth and fifth sons of Japheth (Ge 10:2). Ancient Moshi/Mushki and Tubalu/Tibareni people dwelled south of the Black and Caspian Seas in Ezekiel's time. Today, these nations are Turkey and possibly south Russia and northern Iran.
- **Beth-Togarmah** is the third son of **Gomer**, Japheth's first son (Ge 10:3). Ezekiel 38:6 says that Beth-Togarmah is from the remote parts of the north with all its troops. Togarmah, therefore, is to the far north of Israel.
- **Madai** is the third son of Japheth and became the Medes (Gen 10:2). The Medes settled in the Caspian Sea until Cyrus defeated the Medes and they remained in the province of Persia.
- **Persia** has its earliest roots to the Indo-Aryans as early as 2000 BC and settled along the Black Sea coast. The Persian empire today is Iran. Persia was changed to Iran in March 1935 and in 1979 became the Islamic Republic of Iran.
- **Javan** was the fourth son of Japheth and was the father of the Ionians, or Greeks (Gen 10:2)
- **Tiras** was the seventh son of Japheth father of the ancient Thracians, later known as Tarshish which is Spain where Jonah had headed (Jonah 1:1–3; Ge 10:4).

The generation of **Ham** (Arabians) separated from God and went to live in Cush, Mizraim, Put and Canaan (Ge 10:6).

- **Cush** today is Sudan (Ethiopia and Somalia). The sons of Cush were Seba, Havilah, Sabtah, Raamah, and Sabtechah; the sons of Raamah were Sheba and Dedan (today Saudi Arabia). Cush begot Nimrod, and the beginning of his kingdom was Babel (Babylon), Erech, Accad, and Calneh in the land of Shinar (Iraq). From there, he went to Assyria and built Nineveh, Rehoboth, Ir, Calah, and Resen between Nineveh and Calah (Ge 10:6–12).
- **Mizraim** today is Egypt. Mizraim begot Ludim, Anamin, Lehabim, Naphtuhim, Pathrusim, and Casluhim, from whom came the Philistines and Caphtorim (Ge 10:13–14).

- **Put** today is Libya. Put is west of Egypt in Africa under Muamaar Qaddafi since 1969.
- **Canaan** became Palestine. Palestine today continues to initiate terrorism against Israel. The PLO (Palestinian Liberation Organization), the NIF (National Islamic Front), and PAIC (Popular Arab and Islamic Conference) are extremist Islamic forces against Israel.

Who Will Come to Save the Day?

> Rev 19:11 *Now I saw heaven opened, and behold, a white horse. And He who sat on him was called Faithful and True, and in righteousness He judges and makes war.* 12a *His eyes were like a flame of fire, and on His head were many crowns.*

Presley[6] helps us understand the many crowns depicted in verse 12, "The Greek word for crowns here is diadem which symbolizes royalty, sovereign rule and dominion. The many crowns that Christ is seen wearing here in His approach from heaven will be the crowns of all of the kingdoms that ever existed until His return. The only reason the word *many* is used instead of *all* at this time is that there will yet be a future kingdom of Satan at the end of the Millennial Kingdom. Christ will have to defeat that final worldwide kingdom that will attack Israel at that time before the eternal state in heaven of all who are saved can become reality (Rev 20:7–10). But Christ will indeed conquer that final worldly kingdom on the regenerated earth as well, for Jesus Christ is already King of kings even now. Most people just do not yet know it."

> Rev 19:12b *He had a name written that no one knew except Himself.* 13 *He was clothed with a robe dipped in blood, and His name is called The Word of God.* 14 *And the armies in heaven, clothed in fine linen, white and clean, followed Him on white horses.* 15 *Now out of His mouth goes a sharp sword, that with it He should strike the nations. And He Himself will rule them with a rod of iron. He Himself treads the winepress of the fierceness and wrath of Almighty God.* 16 *And He has on His robe and on*

> *His thigh a name written: KING OF KINGS AND LORD OF LORDS.[17]Then I saw an angel standing in the sun; and he cried with a loud voice, saying to all the birds that fly in the midst of heaven, "Come and gather together for the supper of the great God, [18]that you may eat the flesh of kings, the flesh of captains, the flesh of mighty men, the flesh of horses and of those who sit on them, and the flesh of all people, free and slave, both small and great." [19]And I saw the beast, the kings of the earth, and their armies, gathered together to make war against Him who sat on the horse and against His army. [20a]Then the beast was captured, and with him the false prophet who worked signs in his presence, by which he deceived those who received the mark of the beast and those who worshiped his image.*

❖ Zechariah 14 shows the events of the Lord when He comes back to win the battle.

The Scripture for the actual Battle of Armageddon is in Zechariah 14 and ends with the Antichrist and the Antispirit being cast into the lake of fire. Let's cover all of Zechariah 14 in detail – it is called, "The Day of the Lord."

- Zec 14:1–2a: "Behold, the day of the Lord is coming, And your spoil will be divided in your midst. For I will gather all the nations to battle against Jerusalem;"

All the armies of the world will gather in Jerusalem.

- Zec 2b: "The city shall be taken, The houses rifled, And the women ravished. Half of the city shall go into captivity, But the remnant of the people shall not be cut off from the city."

Jerusalem will be invaded by the Antichrist and his army. Half the city shall be taken into captivity with their houses being invaded and women ravished. Without the return of Christ, God's people would be annihilated.

- Zec 14:3–4: "Then the Lord will go forth And fight against those nations, As He fights in the day of battle. And in that day His feet will stand on the Mount of Olives, Which faces Jerusalem on the east. And the Mount of Olives shall be split in two, from east to west, Making a very large valley; Half of the mountain shall move toward the north And half of it toward the south."

Christ will return on His white charger and all the saints with Him on their white horses. As He steps on the Mount of Olives, it will split in two from east to west. It will give a way for the army to flee and a way for the Jews to be protected from the Antichrist. This will fulfill the Rosh Hashanah (Feast of Trumpets) for the Jews. The next Jewish feast will be the Ten Days of Awe. Jesus will be busy during this time.

- Zec 14:5a: "Then you shall flee through My mountain valley, For the mountain valley shall reach to Azal. Yes, you shall flee As you fled from the earthquake In the days of Uzziah king of Judah."

The army of the Antichrist will flee from Jerusalem to the Jezreel Valley or valley of Megiddo.

- Zec 14:5b–7: "Thus the Lord my God will come, And all the saints with You. It shall come to pass in that day That there will be no light; The lights will diminish. It shall be one day Which is known to the Lord—Neither day nor night. But at evening time it shall happen That it will be light."

The sun had burned out so that when the light comes into darkness, the people will be blinded at first until they get accustomed to the light.

- Zec 14:8–9: "And in that day it shall be That living waters shall flow from Jerusalem, Half of them toward the eastern sea And half of them toward the western sea; In both summer and winter it shall occur. And the Lord shall be King over all the earth. In that day it shall be—'The Lord is one,' And His name one."

The seas were contaminated with blood and dead sea creatures. Living waters will flow from Messiah's throne room in Jerusalem. The eastern sea is the Dead Sea, and the western sea is the Mediterranean. Living waters always represent the Holy Spirit bringing life to everything. A representation of Jerusalem in heaven will be brought to earth. Jesus will reign as King of Kings and Lord of Lords. Everyone shall bow at the mention of the name of Jesus.

- Zec 14:10: "All the land shall be turned into a plain from Geba to Rimmon south of Jerusalem. Jerusalem shall be raised up and inhabited in her place from Benjamin's Gate to the place of the First Gate and the Corner Gate, and from the Tower of Hananel to the king's winepresses."

The topography will change and the plain extends from Geba in the north of Jerusalem to Rimmon in the south.

- Zec 14:11: "The people shall dwell in it; And no longer shall there be utter destruction, But Jerusalem shall be safely inhabited."

The promises of God have been fulfilled. God's people can now live safely in Jerusalem.

- Zec 14:12: "And this shall be the plague with which the Lord will strike all the people who fought against Jerusalem: Their flesh shall dissolve while they stand on their feet, their eyes shall dissolve in their sockets, and their tongues shall dissolve in their mouths."

Then the Lord goes north out of Jerusalem to Megiddo for the Battle of Armageddon that has been forming and with the sword of the Lord strikes the enemy warring against Israel.

- Zec 14:13–14: "It shall come to pass in that day That a great panic from the Lord will be among them. Everyone will seize the hand of his neighbor, And raise his hand against his neighbor's hand; Judah also will fight at Jerusalem. And the wealth of all the surrounding nations Shall be gathered together: Gold, silver, and apparel in great abundance."

It looks as though the Israelites living in Jerusalem will need to take possession of their property. The spoil or wealth of the enemy is gathered by the homeowners. When the battle is over, ten days after His return, Jesus will enter through the Eastern Gate with His saints. On the Day of Atonement (Yom Kippur) Christ will enter the Holy of Holies to rule as King of Kings and Lord of Lords.

- Zec 14:15: "Such also shall be the plague On the horse and the mule, On the camel and the donkey, And on all the cattle that will be in those camps. So shall this plague be."

The horse, mule, camel, donkey, and cattle are the weapons and artillery of the enemy seen by John during the battle. Jesus does not have worldly weapons, but fights with spiritual warfare.

- Zec 14:16–19: "And it shall come to pass that everyone who is left of all the nations which came against Jerusalem shall go up from year to year to worship the King, the Lord of hosts, and to keep the Feast of Tabernacles. And it shall be that whichever of the families of the earth do not come up to Jerusalem to worship the King, the Lord of hosts, on them there will be no rain. If the family of Egypt will not come up and enter in, they shall have no rain; they shall receive the plague with which the Lord strikes the nations who do not come up to keep the Feast of Tabernacles. This shall be the punishment of Egypt and the punishment of all the nations that do not come up to keep the Feast of Tabernacles."

Sukkot, the Feast of Tabernacles, will be celebrated on the fifteenth day of the month. The feasts will be reinstated, as well as the sacrificial offerings as a memorial. Everyone must come to worship in Jerusalem. Christ will rule with a theocratic government, ruling with an iron rod.

- Zec 14:20–21: "In that day 'HOLINESS TO THE LORD' shall be engraved on the bells of the horses. The pots in the Lord's house shall be like the bowls before the altar. Yes, every pot in Jerusalem and Judah shall be holiness to the Lord of hosts. Everyone who sacrifices shall come and take them and cook in them. In that day there shall no longer be a Canaanite in the house of the Lord of hosts."

Exodus 28:36 required the high priest to have the words "Holiness unto the Lord" inscribed on his miter. When the temple is erected, the priests will be reinstated for temple worship. The pots and other articles in the sanctuary will be sanctified and made holy as they were in the Old Testament. This will not be a time of living in the flesh but in the spirit of holiness. This is the testing time during the millennium to earn a place in eternity just as today we are earning our place to rule and reign with Christ during the millennium. Our rewards come from obedience to the Holy Spirit.

7. Antichrist and Antispirit are Cast into the Lake of Fire (Rev 19:20b–21)

> [20b]*These two were cast alive into the Lake of Fire burning with brimstone.* [21]*And the rest were killed with the sword which proceeded from the mouth of Him who sat on the horse. And all the birds were filled with their flesh.*

According to Daniel 12:11-12, the second half of the tribulation is over after 1,290 days, but a new figure is interjected here of 1,345 days. This must be the 45 days it will take to go from the day Jesus returned to the day the millennium begins. There is so much for the Holy Spirit to rebuild in Jerusalem; first, the city and then the temple itself. Once the temple is built, Christ will be seated to judge those who lived through the tribulation. Here is where He will judge Satan, the Antichrist, and the False Prophet.

- Da 12:11-12: "And from the time that the daily sacrifice is taken away, and the abomination of desolation is set up, there shall be one thousand two hundred and ninety days. Blessed is he who waits, and comes to the one thousand three hundred and thirty-five days."

Jesus will have fulfilled all of the Jewish feasts that were explained in Leviticus 23. The first three feasts were in the spring, the second in the summer, and the third in the fall. The first three feasts represent Jesus at His first coming in the spring, the creation of the church in the summer, and in the fall, He is represented in His second coming.

Feast	Date	Jewish Holiday	Christian Event/ Holiday
Passover	Beginning of Jewish calendar—14th day	Nisan	celebration of Easter, crucifixion
Unleavened Bread	15th day for 7 days	Zif	confession/sin forgiven
Firstfruits	Day after Sabbath for 7 Sabbaths (7 x 7 = 49)	Sivan	Salvation
Weeks	50th day	Law of God	Pentecost; Spirit of God
Trumpets	7th month, 1st day (30 days to a month)	Rosh Hashanah New Year	second coming
Day of Atonement	10th day, 7th month	Yom Kippur	judgment/pardon
Tabernacles	15th day, 7th month	Sukkot	millennium reign

1. Passover began in Egypt as the beginning of the Jewish calendar. Jesus fulfilled this feast when He became the Passover Lamb for those believers who have faith in Him for salvation.
2. The Feast of Unleavened Bread meant no sin during the next seven days as they were a holy convocation time. They were

to offer a sacrifice for seven days following the Passover. Jesus became our sacrifice for sin.

3. The Feast of Firstfruits was to bring the first of their harvest. Jesus became our firstfruit (1Co 15:20).
4. Pentecost is the fiftieth day, which is a time to be liberated. The fiftieth year is also a jubilee, a year to celebrate liberty, freedom and deliverance from bondage. The church was born on Pentecost. Jesus Christ is the Deliverer.
5. Rosh Hashanah or the Feast of Trumpets was in the fall, which began a new year (like a fiscal year—new time to be blessed). This is the return of Christ (rapture) for a new beginning.
6. Yom Kippur is ten days later, the Day of Atonement, the day of national cleansing. These ten days will be a time of judgment for the people who lived through the tribulation.
7. Sukkot or the Feast of Tabernacles comes five days later. This is a day of celebration for the Jews for their freedom from Egypt. This will forever be a time of celebration as it welcomes the new millennium. The millennium does not begin until the forty-fifth day according to Daniel 12:12.

CHAPTER 10

Revelation 20: Millennial Rule by Christ

This is a new dispensation. The first dispensation in the New Testament was the church age. Then we saw the tribulation age. Now we will see the millennial age.

1. Third Judgment—Satan is Judged – Bound 1,000 Years (Rev 20:1–3)
2. Fourth Judgment—Nations are Judged (Rev 20:4a)
3. Resurrection of the Dead (Rev 20:4b–6a)
4. Christ Reigns During the Millennium (Rev 20:6b)
5. Satan is Loosed (Rev 20:7–8)
6. Satan is Cast Into the Lake of Fire (Rev 20:9-10)
7. Fifth Judgment—All are Judged—Great White Throne Judgment (Rev 20:11–15)

1. Third Judgment—Satan is Judged—Bound 1,000 Years (Rev 20:1–3)

> [1]*Then I saw an angel coming down from heaven, having the key to the bottomless pit and a great chain in his hand.* [2]*He laid hold of the dragon, that serpent of old, who is the Devil and Satan, and bound him for a thousand years;* [3]*and he cast him into the bottomless pit, and shut him up, and set a seal on him, so that he should deceive the nations no more till the thousand years were finished. But after these things he must be released for a little while.*

Satan will be bound for a thousand years while Jesus rules (Da 7:9; Isa 61:6; 1Co 6:2–3). Don't think of this as a physical chain but whatever chain would bind a spirit. The bottomless pit or the abyss or Hades refers to the place where demons are bound (2Pe 1–10; Jude 7). Revelation 1:18 says Jesus has the key to death and Hades.

Satan here is called the dragon, the serpent of old, and the Devil. No matter the name, Satan will be bound for a thousand years so he cannot deceive the nations. And it doesn't matter if Satan is present or not, humanity will continue to sin, which is its nature.

- Isa 11:9: "They shall not hurt nor destroy in all My holy mountain, for the earth shall be full of the knowledge of the LORD as the waters cover the sea."
- Da 6:17: "Then a stone was brought and laid on the mouth of the den, and the king sealed it with his own signet ring and with the signets of his lords, that the purpose concerning Daniel might not be changed."
- Zec 14:16: "And it shall come to pass that everyone who is left of all the nations which came against Jerusalem shall go up from year to year to worship the King, the LORD of hosts, and to keep the Feast of Tabernacles."
- Ro 11:26-27: "And so all Israel will be saved, as it is written: 'The Deliverer will come out of Zion, and He will turn away ungodliness from Jacob; For this is My covenant with them, when I take away their sins.'"
- 2Pe 2:4: "For if God did not spare the angels who sinned, but cast them down to hell and delivered them into chains of darkness, to be reserved for judgment..."

2. Fourth Judgment—Nations Are Judged (Rev 20:4a)

> [4a]*And I saw thrones, and they sat on them, and judgment was committed to them.*

This is the first sheep/goat judgment spoken of in Matthew 25. First, Jesus judges those who will live through the millennium, and secondly, He judges those who will live through eternity after His thousand-year rule. Jesus will judge their hearts. Those who live in the millennial rule will have to succumb to an iron rule by Christ, yet they will have children, and after the millennium, many will rise up against Christ.

Also, those living under Christ have always had to believe He was the Messiah, and this will be the case here. According to the Matthew 25 prophecy, it is still based on faith. It cannot be on works because Ephesians 2:8–9 says humanity cannot please God based on good works. The Messiah chose those who supported others; He saw that as goodness, and all goodness comes from God. Jesus died on the cross to redeem all people, and these will receive grace from God just as every other human being.

- Da 7:9: "I watched till Thrones were put in place, and the Ancient of Days was seated…"
- 1Co 6:2–3: "Do you not know that the saints will judge the world? And if the world will be judged by you, are you unworthy to judge the smallest matters? Do you not know that we shall judge angels? How much more, things that pertain to this life?"
- Mt 25:31–46: "When the Son of Man comes in His glory, and all the holy angels with Him, then He will sit on the Throne of His glory. All the nations will be gathered before Him, and He will separate them one from another, as a shepherd divides his sheep from the goats. And He will set the sheep on His right hand, but the goats on the left. Then the King will say to those on His right hand, 'Come, you blessed of My Father, inherit the kingdom prepared for you from the foundation of the world: for I was hungry and you gave Me food; I was thirsty and you gave Me drink; I was a stranger and you took Me in; I was naked and you clothed Me; I was sick and you visited Me; I was in prison and you came to Me.' Then the righteous will answer Him, saying, 'Lord, when did we see You hungry and feed You, or thirsty and give You drink? When did we see You a stranger and take You in, or naked and clothe You? Or when did we see You sick, or in prison, and come to You?' And the King will answer and say to them, 'Assuredly, I say to you, inasmuch as you did it to one of the

least of these My brethren, you did it to Me.' Then He will also say to those on the left hand, 'Depart from Me, you cursed, into the everlasting fire prepared for the devil and his angels: for I was hungry and you gave Me no food; I was thirsty and you gave Me no drink; I was a stranger and you did not take Me in, naked and you did not clothe Me, sick and in prison and you did not visit Me.' Then they also will answer Him, saying, 'Lord, when did we see You hungry or thirsty or a stranger or naked or sick or in prison, and did not minister to You?' Then He will answer them, saying, 'Assuredly, I say to you, inasmuch as you did not do it to one of the least of these, you did not do it to Me.' And these will go away into everlasting punishment, but the righteous into eternal life."

3. Resurrection of the Dead (Rev 20:4b–6a)

> [4b]*Then I saw the souls of those who had been beheaded for their witness to Jesus and for the word of God, who had not worshiped the beast or his image, and had not received his mark on their foreheads or on their hands. And they lived and reigned with Christ for a thousand years.* [5]*But the rest of the dead did not live again until the thousand years were finished. This is the first resurrection.* [6a]*Blessed and holy is he who has part in the first resurrection. Over such the second death has no power, but they shall be priests of God and of Christ, and shall reign with Him a thousand years.*

Here, we see the martyrs who were resurrected and are now around the throne. It seems they have become part of the church who will rule and reign with Christ during the millennium. At the end of the millennium, we will have a resurrection at the great white throne judgment to see who lives for eternity. Those that were a part of the first resurrection (the church) will not have to be judged at the great white throne judgment.

It is difficult to visualize a resurrected body. Paul tells us in 1 Corinthians 15:50 that flesh and blood cannot enter the kingdom of God, yet the resurrected body must have a framework of bones because Ezekiel says the dry bones come back together. In my small mind, I just see a spiritual body and a flesh body. The flesh body cannot go to heaven; only the spiritual body can. However, the spirit body must be visible because when Jesus appeared to the disciples after His resurrection in Luke 24:37, the disciples could see and touch Him.

- 1Co 15:51–53: "Behold, I tell you a mystery: We shall not all sleep, but we shall all be changed— in a moment, in the twinkling of an eye, at the last trumpet. For the trumpet will sound, and the dead will be raised incorruptible, and we shall be changed. For this corruptible must put on incorruption, and this mortal must put on immortality."

4. Christ Reigns during the Millennium (Rev 20:6b)

> [6b]*but they shall be priests of God and of Christ, and shall reign with Him a thousand years.*

Ezekiel 40–46 describes the temple that will be established in Jerusalem during the millennium. The structure is of a city. The sacrificial system will be instituted again, but this is a mystery. In Hebrews 10:12, Christ offered one sacrifice for the forgiveness of sins forever. During this period of grace, there has been no need for a Christian to call upon any other sacrifice but Jesus Christ's. In the millennium, Christ will be present for all to see. Yet today, Christ requires us to have communion to remember His sacrificial death. Maybe the sacrificial system during the millennium will be reinstated because being involved in the act of substituting an animal is more vivid and difficult as an evidence of faith.

- Josh 3:5: "And Joshua said to the people, 'Sanctify yourselves, for tomorrow the LORD will do wonders among you.'"
- Jer 30:9: "But they shall serve the LORD their God, and David their king, Whom I will raise up for them."
- Ez 34:24: "And I, the LORD, will be their God, and My servant David a prince among them; I, the LORD, have spoken."
- Ez 37:25: "Then they shall dwell in the land that I have given to Jacob My servant, where your fathers dwelt; and they shall dwell

there, they, their children, and their children's children, forever; and My servant David shall be their prince forever."

- Ez 44:1–3: "Then He brought me back to the outer gate of the sanctuary which faces toward the east, but it was shut. And the Lord said to me, 'This gate shall be shut; it shall not be opened, and no man shall enter by it, because the Lord God of Israel has entered by it; therefore it shall be shut. As for the prince, because he is the prince, he may sit in it to eat bread before the Lord; he shall enter by way of the vestibule of the gateway, and go out the same way.'"
- Ez 44:23: "And they [priests] shall teach My people the difference between the holy and the unholy, and cause them to discern between the unclean and the clean."

Ezekiel 45:1-8 says a district of land is set apart for the Lord, the government, and the priests. The prince is portioned a piece of land to the left and right of these districts. Verses 18-25 say the feasts are to be kept. Ezekiel 48 showed the division of the land amongst the twelve tribes. These were not the same as mentioned previously in the Bible.

- Judah and Benjamin surround the city; they remained faithful in the divided kingdom.
- Joseph and Benjamin were born to Rachel.
- Joseph's children, Manasseh and Ephraim, inherit.
- Ruben, Simeon, Levi, Judah, Issachar, and Zebulun were Leah's children.
- Levi's children were the priests.
- Dan and Naphtali were born to Rachel's handmaiden, Bilhah.
- Gad and Asher were born to Leah's handmaiden, Zilpar.
- The handmaiden's children were placed the farthest away from the temple.

5. Satan Is Loosed (Rev 20:7–9a)

> *[7]Now when the thousand years have expired, Satan will be released from his prison [8]and will go out to deceive the nations*

> *which are in the four corners of the earth, Gog and Magog, to gather them together to battle, whose number is as the sand of the sea.* [9a]*They went up on the breadth of the earth and surrounded the camp of the saints and the beloved city.*

When Satan is released, Satan will be Satan and humanity will be humanity. He always comes to kill, steal, and destroy (Jn 10:10). Satan will persuade many to join him in the battle against God.

6. Satan Is Cast Into the Lake of Fire (Rev 20:9b–10)

> [9b]*And fire came down from God out of heaven and devoured them.* [10]*The devil, who deceived them, was cast into the Lake of Fire and brimstone where the beast and the false prophet are. And they will be tormented day and night forever and ever.*

The battle doesn't happen. Ezekiel says fire from heaven comes upon Magog, the leader of the battle, and he is sent into the lake of fire forever. Good-bye and good riddance.

- Ez 39:6: "And I will send fire on Magog and on those who live in security in the coastlands. Then they shall know that I am the LORD."

7. 5th Judgment—All Are Judged—Great White Throne Judgment (Rev 20:11–15)

> [11]*Then I saw a great white throne and Him who sat on it, from whose face the earth and the heaven fled away. And there was found no place for them.* [12]*And I saw the dead, small and great, standing before God, and books were opened. And another book was opened, which is the Book of Life. And the dead were judged according to their works, by the things which were written in the books.* [13]*The sea gave up the dead who were in it, and Death and Hades delivered up the dead who were in them. And they were judged, each one according to his works.* [14]*Then Death and Hades were cast into the Lake of Fire. This is the*

> *second death. [15]And anyone not found written in the Book of Life was cast into the Lake of Fire.*

In 21:2, New Jerusalem comes down from heaven. In verse 4, He who sat on the throne made everything new. This must be where the great white throne judgment takes place. All people are moved from heaven and earth to this area for judgment because after the judgment ends, the old earth and the old heaven will be cleansed and made new according to Revelation 21:1–2. Then, chapters 21 and 22 tell us how eternity will be run. But first, the Lord eliminates the unrighteous people, ridding anyone not written in the Book of Life to the lake of fire. Those left will be assigned for eternal living with God.

- 2Pe 3:7: "But the heavens and the earth which are now preserved by the same word, are reserved for fire until the day of judgment and perdition of ungodly men."

Death in the Greek is the noun *thanatos*, the separation of the spirit and soul from the body. Death is not a state of nonexistence. The spiritual form in the lake of fire will forever be separated from God and goodness. Death is the consequence of sin, which was brought about by Satan, and all his followers will forever be with their lord Satan.

CHAPTER 11

Revelation 21–22: New Things

Everything created in Genesis was corrupted by Satan and evil. God will recreate everything new just as He did in the time of Noah.

All heaven will celebrate with Christ and His bride (the church). Now is the testimony of the truth of the Word of God. Eternity begins. All things are made new:

1. New Heaven
2. New Earth
3. New Jerusalem
4. New Nations
5. New River of Water of Life
6. New Tree of Life
7. New Throne

The Holy Spirit posed this question to me: Is the new heaven, earth, and Jerusalem one place or three? Many commentaries say that New Jerusalem comes out of heaven and sits on the earth and God has finally come to dwell with His people—that would be one place. I could understand the Trinity coming together in one place throughout eternity. However, that is not the conviction the Holy Spirit is giving me. I believe the Bible says three distinct places: a new heaven, a new earth, and a New Jerusalem.

When the great white throne judgment happens, I believe this is New Jerusalem coming out of heaven as a planet bringing forth the light of the Lord upon the earth, as the sun has burned itself out. New Jerusalem is where the throne of God will be. All people will be brought before this judgment—those from the graves, from earth, and from heaven. The unrighteous will be sentenced to the lake of fire for eternity with their lord Satan, and the righteous will be given life for eternity with their Lord Jesus.

When all peoples are in New Jerusalem, the original earth will be destroyed by fire (2Pe 3:7) and the Holy Spirit will renew the earth to the condition that God made it before sin, when He walked in the garden of Eden with Adam. The earth will be made into its eternal condition. Then, the Holy Spirit will purge heaven of sin because Satan defiled everything God made. Only then will God's people go to their perfect, eternal dwelling.

It makes sense that those who received a glorified body and have mansions in heaven will return to the new heaven for their eternal dwelling. The righteous who lived through the millennium will return to the new earth and live eternally in their earthly body.

To understand the difference between glorified and earthly bodies, we must go to 1 Corinthians 15. People will have immortality of soul and spirit according to 1 Peter 3:4 and of body in the resurrection (1Co 15:51–58). Once they are made into spiritual beings having put on incorruption and immortality, their state will not change. Without a resurrection to heaven, those on earth will remain in an earthly body.

New Jerusalem will be where the throne resides. On earth, there will be a temple because Ezekiel 37:26–28 says the temple is forever on the Temple Mount in Jerusalem. There is a difference: throne in New Jerusalem, temple in the city of Jerusalem on earth. This is why I cannot agree that New Jerusalem comes to the earth. There is no throne on the earth. David will be king in Israel and rule from this temple (Ez 34:22–24). Jesus is King of Kings. Jesus told the woman at the well in John 4, "The hour is coming when you will neither on this mountain, nor in Jerusalem, worship the Father …[23] But the hour is coming, and now is, when the true worshipers will worship the Father in spirit and truth; for the Father is seeking such to worship Him. [24] God is Spirit, and those who worship Him must worship in spirit and truth."

Those in heaven will be able to move by thought to come to New Jerusalem to worship Jesus in the throne room because 21:25 says the gates shall not be shut. Since those with an earthly body went to New Jerusalem for the white throne judgment, it is likely they will be transformed to also travel by thought. Perhaps our next kingdom is a universal kingdom. In spite of all my research, I know there are still so many hidden treasures. My earthly body can never comprehend the many gifts my glorified body will contain.

Let's read the Bible text to see how this plays out in detail.

1. New Heaven (Rev 21:1a)

> [1a]*Now I saw a new heaven.*

According to Isaiah 65 and 2 Peter, the heavens and earth won't be done away with but purged of sin from anywhere Satan caused pollution.

- Isa 65:17–19: "For behold, I create new heavens and a new earth; and the former shall not be remembered or come to mind. But be glad and rejoice forever in what I create; for behold, I create Jerusalem as a rejoicing, and her people a joy. I will rejoice in Jerusalem and joy in My people; the voice of weeping shall no longer be heard in her, nor the voice of crying."
- 2Pe 3:7–13: "But the heavens and the earth which are now preserved by the same word, are reserved for fire until the day of judgment and perdition of ungodly men. But, beloved, do not forget this one thing, that with the Lord one day is as a thousand years, and a thousand years as one day. The Lord is not slack concerning His promise, as some count slackness, but is longsuffering toward us, not willing that any should perish but that all should come to repentance. But the day of the Lord will come as a thief in the night, in which the heavens will pass away with a great noise, and the elements will melt with fervent heat; both the earth and the works that are in it will be burned up. Therefore, since all these things will be dissolved, what manner of persons ought you to be in holy conduct and godliness, looking for and hastening the coming of the day of God, because of which the heavens will be dissolved, being on fire, and the elements will melt with fervent

heat? Nevertheless we, according to His promise, look for new heavens and a new earth in which righteousness dwells."

2. New Earth (Rev 21:1b)

> [1b]*and a new earth, for the first heaven and the first earth had passed away. Also there was no more sea.*

Daniel 2:44 prophesied that God's kingdom would never be destroyed and that David would reign on the throne forever. Notice that there will be no more sea upon the earth. Our minds can't comprehend what a great paradise the Lord has waiting for us. I believe it will be restored to its original condition when Adam and Eve walked in the garden with the Lord. God said in Genesis 1:26, let us create man in our image. This image is the spirit. Then in verse 28, God said to be fruitful and multiply His spirit upon the face of the earth. We are to be fruitful and take on the image of the fruit of the spirit in Galatians 5:22. That is how I picture the new earth—exactly how God created it to be.

3. New Jerusalem (Rev 21:2–23)

> [2]*Then I, John, saw the holy city, New Jerusalem, coming down out of heaven from God, prepared as a bride adorned for her husband.*

New Jerusalem comes down to be a planet by itself; it is the location of the throne of God and gives light to the universe and especially to the earth as the sun has burned itself out. We see a new heaven (home to the bride of Christ) and a new earth (home to humankind). Our text says that the bride is New Jerusalem. New Jerusalem will be the seat for the government of God's kingdom that is ruled from the throne of God.

- Isa 52:1: "Awake, awake! Put on your strength, O Zion; put on your beautiful garments, O Jerusalem, the holy city! For the uncircumcised and the unclean shall no longer come to you."

- Zec 8:8: "I will bring them back, and they shall dwell in the midst of Jerusalem. They shall be My people and I will be their God, in truth and righteousness."

> *3And I heard a loud voice from heaven saying, "Behold, the tabernacle of God is with men, and He will dwell with them, and they shall be His people. God Himself will be with them and be their God."*

The tabernacle of David will be on the new earth, where God will return to be the Shekinah glory for His people.

- Lev 26:11: "I will set My Tabernacle among you, and My soul shall not abhor you."

> *4And God will wipe away every tear from their eyes; there shall be no more death, nor sorrow, nor crying. There shall be no more pain, for the former things have passed away.*

The author continues to describe life on earth with God present. The law of sin and death is gone forever.

> *5Then He who sat on the throne said, "Behold, I make all things new." And He said to me, "Write, for these words are true and faithful."*

- 2Pe 3:13: "Nevertheless we, according to His promise, look for new heavens and a new earth in which righteousness dwells."

Jesus now speaks from the throne of God in New Jerusalem. According to Peter, the new heaven and the new earth is where the righteous dwell. New Jerusalem is the throne room. Earthly people dwell on the new earth, and glorified people dwell in the new heaven.

> *6And He said to me, "It is done! I am the Alpha and the Omega, the Beginning and the End. I will give of the fountain of the*

water of life freely to him who thirsts. [7]He who overcomes shall inherit all things, and I will be his God and he shall be My son. [8]But the cowardly, unbelieving, abominable, murderers, sexually immoral, sorcerers, idolaters, and all liars shall have their part in the lake which burns with fire and brimstone, which is the second death."

Remember in chapters 2 and 3 that the overcomers will inherit the kingdom of God. Here it is, another promise of God comes true.

- Isa 25:8: "He will swallow up death forever, and the Lord GOD will wipe away tears from all faces; the rebuke of His people He will take away from all the earth; for the LORD has spoken."

[9]Then one of the seven angels who had the seven bowls filled with the seven last plagues came to me and talked with me, saying, "Come, I will show you the bride, the Lamb's wife."
[10] And he carried me away in the Spirit to a great and high mountain, and showed me the great city, the holy Jerusalem, descending out of heaven from God, [11]having the glory of God. Her light was like a most precious stone, like a jasper stone, clear as crystal. [12]Also she had a great and high wall with twelve gates, and twelve angels at the gates, and names written on them, which are the names of the twelve tribes of the children of Israel: [13]three gates on the east, three gates on the north, three gates on the south, and three gates on the west. [14]Now the wall of the city had twelve foundations, and on them were the names of the twelve apostles of the Lamb.
[15]And he who talked with me had a gold reed to measure the city, its gates, and its wall. [16]The city is laid out as a square; its length is as great as its breadth. And he measured the city with the reed: twelve thousand furlongs. Its length, breadth, and height are equal. [17]Then he measured its wall: one hundred and forty-four cubits, according to the measure of a man, that is, of an angel. [18]The construction of its wall was of jasper; and the city was pure gold, like clear glass. [19]The foundations

of the wall of the city were adorned with all kinds of precious stones: the first foundation was jasper, the second sapphire, the third chalcedony, the fourth emerald, [20]the fifth sardonyx, the sixth sardius, the seventh chrysolite, the eighth beryl, the ninth topaz, the tenth chrysoprase, the eleventh jacinth, and the twelfth amethyst. [21]The twelve gates were twelve pearls: each individual gate was of one pearl. And the street of the city was pure gold, like transparent glass.

Oden Hetrick's *Inside the City Gates* includes a description of the holy city of Jerusalem as seen when he was taken to heaven over eighty times in the spirit and reflects this same description here in Revelation. It has become one of those books I give as presents to anyone who has lost a loved one because of the awe-inspiring picture of where their loved ones now reside. I recommend it highly.

- Isa 54:11: "O you afflicted one, tossed with tempest, and not comforted, behold, I will lay your stones with colorful gems, and lay your foundations with sapphires."

[22]But I saw no temple in it, for the Lord God Almighty and the Lamb are its temple. [23]The city had no need of the sun or of the moon to shine in it, for the glory of God illuminated it. The Lamb is its light.

New Jerusalem replaces the sun that has burned itself out with God's Shekinah glory.

- Isa 60:20: "Your sun shall no longer go down, nor shall your moon withdraw itself; for the LORD will be your everlasting light, and the days of your mourning shall be ended."

4. New Nations (Rev 21:24–27)

[24]And the nations of those who are saved shall walk in its light, and the kings of the earth bring their glory and honor into it.

> [25]*Its gates shall not be shut at all by day (there shall be no night there).* [26]*And they shall bring the glory and the honor of the nations into it.* [27]*But there shall by no means enter it anything that defiles, or causes an abomination or a lie, but only those who are written in the Lamb's Book of Life.*

There will be new nations and new rulers within God's kingdom dispatched to rule over them.

Perhaps the gates will never be shut because those in their new body will be able to move from the new heaven to the new earth and New Jerusalem and even beyond to other planets. When we get there, God will reveal the purpose of our new kingdom. God accomplished His plan. This is the final fulfillment of Immanuel, God with us. God's throne has been in heaven ever since He created it, but now that the new earth has been purified by fire, God can dwell among His people.

It was mandatory for Jews to go to the temple in Jerusalem at least three times a year for the Feasts of Passover (spring), Feast of Weeks (summer) and the Feast of Tabernacles (fall). If an earthly body has access to New Jerusalem, it would make sense that they would go to New Jerusalem for these feasts. Or they would be required to go to the temple on earth to celebrate these feasts. In Leviticus 23, where the feasts are explained, they are the feasts of the Lord, not just for the Jews. In 2 Chronicles 2:4, we read, "Behold, I am building a temple for the name of the Lord my God, to dedicate it to Him, to burn before Him sweet incense, for the continual showbread, for the burnt offerings morning and evening, on the Sabbaths, on the New Moons, and on the set feasts of the Lord our God. This is an ordinance forever to Israel."

In God's economy, it makes sense that these feasts will continue to be memorialized for eternity. I can't think of anything that would be more important than celebrating and worshiping the Lord. I even think it will be our greatest pastime.

- Joel 3:17: "So you shall know that I am the LORD your God, dwelling in Zion My holy mountain. Then Jerusalem shall be holy, and no aliens shall ever pass through her again."

- Jn 4:23: "But the hour is coming, and now is, when the true worshipers will worship the Father in spirit and truth; for the Father is seeking such to worship Him."
- Phil 4:3: "And I urge you also, true companion, help these women who labored with me in the Gospel, with Clement also, and the rest of my fellow workers, whose names are in the Book of Life."

5. New River of Water of Life (Rev 22:1)

> [1]*And he showed me a pure river of water of life, clear as crystal, proceeding from the throne of God and of the Lamb.*

The new river of Water of Life is a picture of eternal life flowing. This River of Life always flowed through the Holy Spirit from the throne room of God to His people. The garden of Eden also had this river of Water of Life flowing through it. Jesus Christ is the Water of Life in John 7:37.

- Jn 4:7–14: "A woman of Samaria came to draw water. Jesus said to her, 'Give Me a drink.' For His disciples had gone away into the city to buy food. Then the woman of Samaria said to Him, 'How is it that You, being a Jew, ask a drink from me, a Samaritan woman?' For Jews have no dealings with Samaritans. Jesus answered and said to her, 'If you knew the gift of God, and who it is who says to you, "Give Me a drink," you would have asked Him, and He would have given you living water.' The woman said to Him, 'Sir, You have nothing to draw with, and the well is deep. Where then do You get that living water? Are You greater than our father Jacob, who gave us the well, and drank from it himself, as well as his sons and his livestock?' Jesus answered and said to her, 'Whoever drinks of this water will thirst again, but whoever drinks of the water that I shall give him will never thirst. But the water that I shall give him will become in him a fountain of water springing up into everlasting life.'"
- Ez 47:1–12: "Then he brought me back to the door of the Temple; and there was water, flowing from under the threshold of the Temple toward the east, for the front of the Temple faced east;

the water was flowing from under the right side of the Temple, south of the altar. He brought me out by way of the north gate, and led me around on the outside to the outer gateway that faces east; and there was water, running out on the right side. And when the man went out to the east with the line in his hand, he measured one thousand cubits, and he brought me through the waters; the water came up to my ankles. Again he measured one thousand and brought me through the waters; the water came up to my knees. Again he measured one thousand and brought me through; the water came up to my waist. Again he measured one thousand, and it was a river that I could not cross; for the water was too deep, water in which one must swim, a river that could not be crossed. He said to me, 'Son of man, have you seen this?' Then he brought me and returned me to the bank of the river. When I returned, there, along the bank of the river, were very many trees on one side and the other. Then he said to me: 'This water flows toward the eastern region, goes down into the valley, and enters the sea. When it reaches the sea, its waters are healed. And it shall be that every living thing that moves, wherever the rivers go, will live. There will be a very great multitude of fish, because these waters go there; for they will be healed, and everything will live wherever the river goes. It shall be that fishermen will stand by it from En Gedi to En Eglaim; they will be places for spreading their nets. Their fish will be of the same kinds as the fish of the Great Sea, exceedingly many. But its swamps and marshes will not be healed; they will be given over to salt. Along the bank of the river, on this side and that, will grow all kinds of trees used for food; their leaves will not wither, and their fruit will not fail. They will bear fruit every month, because their water flows from the sanctuary. Their fruit will be for food, and their leaves for medicine.'"

- Jn 7:37–38: "On the last day, that great day of the feast, Jesus stood and cried out, saying, 'If anyone thirsts, let him come to Me and drink. He who believes in Me, as the Scripture has said, out of his heart will flow rivers of living water.'"

6. New Tree of Life (Rev 22:2)

> *[2]In the middle of its street, and on either side of the river, was the tree of life, which bore twelve fruits, each tree yielding its fruit every month. The leaves of the tree were for the healing of the nations.*

The Tree of Life has to be a symbol because it is spoken of singularly, yet there is more than one tree as they are on both sides of the River of Life. It makes sense that each tree bears from its own seed because that is how God created everything—a seed begets its own seed. It says that healing comes from the leaves, so this could represent Christ as the Healer bringing forth wholeness of spirit, soul, and body. Perhaps these leaves when consumed provide special nutrients that fulfill spiritual health.

- Ez 47:12: "Along the bank of the river, on this side and that, will grow all kinds of trees used for food; their leaves will not wither, and their fruit will not fail. They will bear fruit every month, because their water flows from the sanctuary. Their fruit will be for food, and their leaves for medicine."

7. New Throne (Rev 22:3–21)

> *[3]And there shall be no more curse, but the throne of God and of the Lamb shall be in it, and His servants shall serve Him. [4]They shall see His face, and His name shall be on their foreheads. [5]There shall be no night there: They need no lamp nor light of the sun, for the Lord God gives them light. And they shall reign forever and ever.*

This is the last new thing that has been purged from Satan. Visualize this purging: a new heaven, a new earth, a New Jerusalem, new nations, new river of Water of Life, new Tree of Life, and a new throne. It is now that God's work is finished for this Holy Bible, and the time will come when God is ready to proceed with His next work. This foundation had to be laid in order to now rule the rest of the planets and the universe. God always has bigger and better things for us to learn.

- Ge 3:17–19: "Then to Adam He said, 'Because you have heeded the voice of your wife, and have eaten from the tree of which I commanded you, saying, "You shall not eat of it": 'Cursed *is* the ground for your sake; in toil you shall eat of it all the days of your life. Both thorns and thistles it shall bring forth for you, and you shall eat the herb of the field. In the sweat of your face you shall eat bread till you return to the ground, for out of it you were taken; for dust you are, and to dust you shall return.'"
- Ps 36:9: "For with You is the fountain of life; in Your light we see light."
- Da 7:18: "But the saints of the Most High shall receive the kingdom, and possess the kingdom forever, even forever and ever."
- Da 7:27: "Then the kingdom and dominion, and the greatness of the kingdoms under the whole heaven, shall be given to the people, the saints of the Most High. His kingdom is an everlasting kingdom, and all dominions shall serve and obey Him."
- Mt 5:8: "Blessed are the pure in heart, for they shall see God."

> *[6]Then he said to me, "These words are faithful and true." And the Lord God of the holy prophets sent His angel to show His servants the things which must shortly take place. [7]"Behold, I am coming quickly! Blessed is he who keeps the words of the prophecy of this book." [8]Now I, John, saw and heard these things. And when I heard and saw, I fell down to worship before the feet of the angel who showed me these things. [9]Then he said to me, "See that you do not do that. For I am your fellow servant, and of your brethren the prophets, and of those who keep the words of this book. Worship God." [10]And he said to me, "Do not seal the words of the prophecy of this book, for the time is at hand. [11]He who is unjust, let him be unjust still; he who is filthy, let him be filthy still; he who is righteous, let him be righteous still; he who is holy, let him be holy still."*

The author John is beginning his epilogue here. Everything is complete. He ends the same way he did with his gospel, saying that everything he has written is the truth of exactly what the Holy Spirit gave him. The word *soon* doesn't mean imminent but that when it happens, it will happen quickly. The Holy Spirit told Daniel to seal up what he saw in Daniel 12:10. But it is different for John because God wants all to know that in the dispensation of their lives, they are to be prepared.

- Phil 4:3: "And I urge you also, true companion, help these women who labored with me in the Gospel, with Clement also, and the rest of my fellow workers, whose names are in the Book of Life."

> [12]*"And behold, I am coming quickly, and My reward is with Me, to give to everyone according to his work.* [13]*I am the Alpha and the Omega, the Beginning and the End, the First and the Last."* [14]*Blessed are those who do His commandments, that they may have the right to the tree of life, and may enter through the gates into the city.* [15]*But outside are dogs and sorcerers and sexually immoral and murderers and idolaters, and whoever loves and practices a lie.* [16]*"I, Jesus, have sent My angel to testify to you these things in the churches. I am the Root and the Offspring of David, the Bright and Morning Star."* [17]*And the Spirit and the bride say, "Come!" And let him who hears say, "Come!" And let him who thirsts come. Whoever desires, let him take the water of life freely.*

Here, Jesus is giving us an assurance that He will come and will reward His bride for being faithful to Him.

- Isa 40:10: "Behold, the Lord GOD shall come with a strong hand, and His arm shall rule for Him; behold, His reward *is* with Him, and His work before Him."
- Isa 41:4: "Who has performed and done it, calling the generations from the beginning? 'I, the LORD, *am* the first; and with the last I *am* He.'"

- Isa 55:1: "Ho! Everyone who thirsts, come to the waters; and you who have no money, come, buy and eat. Yes, come, buy wine and milk without money and without price."

> [18]*For I testify to everyone who hears the words of the prophecy of this book: If anyone adds to these things, God will add to him the plagues that are written in this book;* [19]*and if anyone takes away from the words of the book of this prophecy, God shall take away his part from the Book of Life, from the holy city, and from the things which are written in this book.*

After ruling for a thousand years on earth, it is finished! The Alpha (beginning as told in Genesis 1:1) and Omega (end as told in Rev 22:19) will complete God's plan (Rev 22:3). Humanity will no longer rebel against God because the curse of Satan is removed (Nu 24:17; Ex 32:33; Isa 55:1). Christ will surrender His perfect kingdom to the Father (1Co 15:24–26). Humanity will remain a naturally imperishable state as God always intended it to be.

- Ex 32:33: "And the Lord said to Moses, 'Whoever has sinned against Me, I will blot him out of My book.'"

> [20]*He who testifies to these things says, "Surely I am coming quickly." Amen. Even so, come, Lord Jesus!* [21]*The grace of our Lord Jesus Christ be with you all. Amen.*

The last thing offered by Jesus is to "Come." This is the same "come" God gave when he ushered Noah into the ark. This "come" is to all humanity. What a beautiful ending—it is truly a new beginning. Come! Come everyone! I want to love you and create a world greater than you could ever imagine! Trust me! Come!

Where is your eternal life? I choose God and am assured that my life is eternally with Him. It is God's promise and plan for my life. I pray that it is for you too.

Hallelujah!

Epilogue

I pray that you enjoyed the revelations from God throughout this book as much as I did when He gave them to me. There is one thing that stands out—that we have to be overcomers in chapters 2 and 3 to enter chapter 4 to celebrate with King Jesus in heaven.

I am a prayer minister in the deliverance ministry; this seems to be the calling God has placed on my life—to share as I pray with others how we can walk in the spirit and overcome the flesh as we abide in Christ through faith. In 1 John 3:6, we read, "Whoever abides in Him does not sin. Whoever sins has neither seen Him nor known Him," and 1 John 5:18 says, "We know that whoever is born of God does not sin; but he who has been born of God keeps himself, and the wicked one does not touch him." These were John's last verses in his epistles to the churches before writing in Revelation that we are to have repentant spirits and be overcomers.

God entitled my ministry *Abiding in Love.* To abide is to have the mind of Christ (1Co 2:16) in order to bring every thought into captivity to the obedience of Christ (2Co 10:5). This is the most important message God gave me many years after understanding the gospel message. We celebrate that we are human and receive negative thoughts because only then can we go to Christ immediately and see how Christ sees our thoughts. We turn those thoughts to Jesus (repenting is turning to see things as Jesus sees them) and then follow through by releasing His love in every situation until we come to see the fruit of His love, joy, and peace.

It takes His patience and kindness to see God's goodness in every thought. Then we can know we have God's faithfulness and can trust and depend on Him to give us His mercy to turn all self-control over to the control of the Holy Spirit.

The fruit of the Spirit is the image of Christ. It is God's love, joy, peace, patience, kindness, goodness, faithfulness, mercy, His gift to have the Holy Spirit in us to help us release ourselves to receive God's control, His will over our lives.

Christians are followers of Christ. Healing comes from His love and presence manifested continuously through faith. The verb *sozo* for salvation means being made into His wholeness moment by moment. The Holy Spirit never leaves us; we can call on Him to be active in us. Abide means moment by moment or continuously. This is true worship of God.

If the Lord tarries, I believe God has another book in me about prayer ministry. God is asking me to share what I am learning in the deliverance ministry. I know that as I write this book, His teachings will be so abounding that I will experience a degree of deliverance that I cannot now comprehend. For me, that is His spiritual enlightenment. Of course, every time I write, it is for my growth and to organize my knowledge in order to teach it. Everything begins with abiding in faith—looking to the Holy Spirit moment by moment to show us how to be delivered from all evil. This is the Lord's Prayer that many pray on a daily basis—deliver us from all evil.

Many of these deliverance principles were placed in my companion book, *Song of Solomon*. While Revelation is the history of Christ taking over His kingship of the kingdom of God, *Song of Solomon* is the story of the bride, the church, and her experiences as she meets Jesus and He woos her to come into covenant with Him. He leaves her with the Holy Spirit, who prepares her for the time when Jesus will come to sweep her off her feet and they are heaven bound. Jesus makes sure she is prepared for every blessing so she can celebrate every step in their relationship together.

Then He introduces her to His Father in heaven, and she receives the blessing of His liquid love. The *Song* continues to show how she matures in heaven during the tribulation to become queen during the millennium to rule and reign with King Jesus. The *Song* stops both times at the sheep/goat judgment. First, at the end of the tribulation, He will fill His bride with wisdom and discernment to know the heart of humanity during the millennium. Then at the next judgment before eternity, Christ actually receives her assessment of the people she ruled over. Again, this is for her as much as the people she had charge over. It is a beautiful story of how much Christ loves, respects, and even glorifies His bride in every way for her to become more and more in His image at every step. Oh that we could take on His image and overcome Satan at every turn! I believe that is why we are left on earth after we receive Christ.

I so look forward to eternity, when I will be filled to overflowing with His light in my glorified body. All the way through the *Song of Solomon*, I could see myself reflect the light of His love. I truly feel in that book, God showed me the growth of a Christian, and I didn't realize when I started that was what God wanted. I was just looking to know His love at a deeper level. Now I know; God wants us all to become overcomers and defeat Satan at every turn because that shows our true worship to God. In return, His love goes deeper and deeper in us.

Thank You, Holy Spirit, for Your guidance in giving me resources. Thank You, Jesus, for the many hours I rested in You and received Your glory before writing the text. Thank You, God—I pray You are pleased and this is truly Your message, not mine. You certainly did not let me release it until You told me it was finished and even gave me direction to go to the next book. How great is our God!

Thank You, Jesus, for giving me purpose in this life. Thank You for being my betrothed, my husband, just as Mary was married to Joseph according to the ancient Jewish wedding even though they had not yet come together. I look to You moment by moment to make me pleasing in God's sight.

Your devoted covenant bride,
Bonnie

Bibliography

1. Aune, David. *Revelation—World Biblical Commentary*. Word, Inc., 1997.
2. Bally, Sherlock. *The Revelation of America in Prophecy*. Logos to Rhema Publishing, 1997.
3. DeYoung, Jimmy. *Daniel: Prophet to the Gentiles*. Shofar Communications, 2013.
4. Larkin, Clarence. *The Book of Revelation*. Forgotten Books, 2007
5. Osborne, Grant R. *Revelation*. Baker Academic, 2002.
6. Presley, Dale M. *Way Truth: Life—Revelation of the Creator LORD Jesus Christ*. 1st Books Library, 1997.

About the Author

Bonnie Westhoff and her husband, Ronnie, worked at the same international corporation while raising their son. In retirement, Bonnie attended Logos Christian College and Graduate School in Jacksonville, Florida, earning her master's in Christian counseling, and her doctorate in ministry/theology. She was ordained in 2003 and currently serves as a healing prayer minister in Jacksonville, Florida. Her son, Ron, and his wife, Jennifer, live in Palmer, Alaska, with her grandchildren, Hollie, Stephanie, and Amy. Her biggest regret in life is that she has lived at the opposite ends of the United States and has missed living close to her grandchildren.

Made in United States
North Haven, CT
10 April 2022

18110431R00129